i

*"I cry out to God Most High,
to God who will fulfill his purpose for me."*

~Psalm 57:2

LIVING
BEYOND
PURPOSE

Stories That Inspire

2019

Contents

Introduction

*M*any times in my life I have been humbled by opportunities to witness God's blessing and miracles; whether in my own life or through the life of a family member, friend or someone else. I cannot and will not profess to know how or why God does what He does, He is after all, God. However, I do know that He is present, and we can experience a glimpse of His love and compassion if we only get to know Him through His son Jesus.

I decided to publish this book because I knew there were others like me who had a story to tell about God's amazing work. Others who had witnessed first-hand his blessings. Normal people like me and like you that had a story of faith to share.

The contributing authors in this book were brave enough to share their own stories and insights. They did this with the hope that other people, like you, would find something to take away. Something that would inspire you to make the important changes in your life. To understand that what you are going through does not define you but can certainly refine you to start living with hope. You can do it; however, you must be willing to believe, take action, and start pursuing your greatest purpose. I would like to tell you that it is going to be easy, but it is not. I would like to say that there is nothing special about the contributors to this book, but that would also not be true. Yet, it would also be false for you to believe that there is nothing special about you, too.

You were created with precision, purpose, and your own unique talents. You were also given the ability to know, act on, and use those talents to become greater and stronger in your own way for God's purposes.

Just accept, remember, and most importantly believe this, "I can do all things through Christ, who strengthens me." Philippians 4:13 (*NKJV*). As I always say, "Through faith and action, ALL things are possible."

Now, let's help YOU start living beyond purpose.

Mike Rodriguez

*"It's not that you don't have a purpose,
you are simply looking in the wrong direction."*
- Mike Rodriguez

Chapter 1

Your Life Is a Gift to You
By Mike Rodriguez

Where you are in your life right now is only temporary, it's up to you to let it become permanent.

This applies to all situations and to all people. Whether you are on top of the world right now, facing a tragic loss or even if you feel that you are just existing, where you are is only temporary. If you are at a point in your life that is not "where" you expected or "what" you expected, that is certainly understandable. It is, however, up to you to let where you are, become permanent. Life doesn't always present good situations, nor are they easy. Regardless of how you view where you are, you must believe that what is happening, is happening for a reason. When facing a tough time or going through a bad situation, let yourself feel whatever emotions you are going through, but don't let them overtake you. Tough times will not last when God is in control.

Most of the challenges that I have lived through, when I trace them back, were usually a result of the consequences of my decisions (or indecisions) which preceded my actions. Yet, I have also learned that God places

1

us in situations or allows situations to happen, for us to get through, so He can get through to us. Situations that you are in may not make sense to you today, but they will later. All of life's experiences serve a higher purpose - to bring us closer to God. He is indeed mysterious and when we seek to understand Him from a human perspective, nothing that has happened or that will happen in our lives could ever make sense, because God is not human. He is the almighty creator of the universe!

In fact, He tells us:

"For My thoughts are not your thoughts,
Nor are your ways My ways," declares the LORD.
"For as the heavens are higher than the earth,
So are My ways higher than your ways
And My thoughts than your thoughts.

– Isaiah 55:8-9

I find that most of us rationalize with and analyze our creator, based on what we feel, want, need or hope to happen. This is where we get side-tracked on our journey through life, especially when we are going through tough times. We must learn to understand that in life, we are either moving closer towards God or we are moving further from Him. Let me clarify that He is always with us and never leaves us. Regardless of where we are in life, what we are doing or what we are going through, he is always there.

When we do things to move further away from God, this means that we are choosing to think, speak or act in a way that is not compatible with allowing Him to go to work in our lives. This usually involves us doing something that we shouldn't be doing, having a lack of faith in general or just living our lives in our own way, according to the world and our will. Awareness of our selfishness creates an awareness of our need to change.

I will be the first one to agree that initially, it will seem very difficult to start making changes in your life that put God first in everything. However, once you make the decision, you will find that living with faith and a positive attitude to change, requires as much energy and effort as living with doubt, worry, fear and uncertainty. Then, once you start trusting Him more, you realize that you can change.

For a large part of my life, although I was a Christian, I had let the ways of the world influence my thoughts, actions and words, which impacted my life plans, which made me look like everyone in this world. We do live in this world, but we should not become like this world. We need to work every day to include Him, not as an add-on, but as "The One." This doesn't mean that you won't have doubts, worries and fears, but it does mean that you can have peace and faith through your tough times. Your life does have a purpose, and there is a light at the end of the tunnel beyond your purpose.

I know that God has always been with me, all the time. There has never been a doubt in my mind. However, I kept Him at a distance to make sure that I didn't feel too bad about my behavior. At times, when I was strong in my faith, I would let my light shine and I felt wonderful. However, when I wasn't strong, when I wasn't living right or when I was just not being happy, I would make sure that I was keeping Him at a reasonable distance. I did this, so I could still feel good about myself. As if He didn't know.

The explanation that I can give is that it was like I was walking through a very long tunnel made of glass, like at an aquarium. The tunnel represented my life's journey. I would walk down the middle of the tunnel and God was ALWAYS walking at the same pace as me, right next to me, but always on the outside of the glass. Not because He wanted to be there, but because I wouldn't let Him in. The glass allowed me to see Him and be assured of His presence, but it also served the purpose of keeping Him from being too close in my life. I wanted His presence, but not His conviction over me, primarily because I was ashamed of my actions. To others, I am also ashamed to say, that I didn't want to come across as "religious." Ironically, when I had low points in my life, I would become angry with God for not being with me. How silly was that thinking, because He was always there.

It was only when I learned to become obedient and change my life, that I finally learned and made the decision to break down that glass wall. We would no longer be separated. I would welcome Him because I was no longer ashamed, and I was empowered by this new amazing and peaceful presence.

His love is unconditional. There is nothing that you have done or that you can do to mess it up. Accept this as a truth and remind yourself of this when you are feeling low.

When you are down, it's easy to feel hopeless and abandoned. Just know that you are never alone, and hope is always present. You only have to believe and seek.

In my new walk, following His purpose, He is still with me and I can still see Him; but now I can feel, know and have a completely different kind of love with Him. There are no barriers between us. The reality is that His love has never changed. Mine has. Most of us live our lives this same way, by using God as a convenience. Sometimes we only call on Him when we are at our darkest moments. It is a truth that no one wants to admit. This is usually apparent when we face some kind of bad or life-changing event, usually with undesirable consequences. He is always there for us, but sometimes we are only there, obediently, when we feel the need or when it is convenient for us. This mindset is counter-productive to building the kind of relationship that we need. Turning away from the ways of the world is very hard indeed.

God made you and me and He knows everything about us and everything that will happen in our lives. We have been prepared for every situation that we will encounter, even when we feel like we can't make it. He loves us unconditionally and wants us all of us, all of the time, good and bad. He wants you to call on Him when you are at your lowest, but He also asks that you praise Him at your highest and all times in between! Give thanks and praise during your good times, but also find the strength to give praise and thanks during difficulties, even when you don't understand what is happening or why it is happening. Of course, this is easier said than done, but it is, in fact, your choice. During good times it's easy to give thanks, yet during difficult times it is equally important to give thanks to God. You are going through whatever it is that you are going through for a reason. He is with you and you must believe that the situation ultimately serves a purpose for His plans for your life.

Life's Standards

There is one constant in life: change will happen. Your life involves people, routines, circumstances, events and God's will. With almost all of these, you have limited power in controlling what happens. What you can control is your faith and your attitude about how you respond to what happens to you. You can also control your decision to act.

Circumstances will happen, and things will not always be in your favor; no one plans on leaving the house and getting in a wreck, but it happens. You might go into work and find out that you have suddenly been laid off, or you might get the surprise gift of a promotion. Things will happen to you, but they are not the standards in your life. They are merely events happening according to events, people, circumstances and of course, God's will.

To better explain how you should view this as you progress in life, I have created a graph. As you look at the graph, you will notice that there are three lines. These lines represent measurements, highs and lows, of where you are when events happen in your life, with examples.

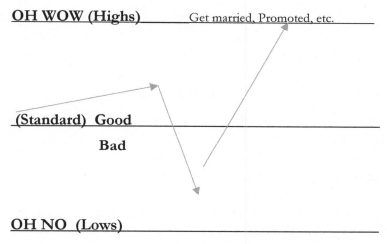

OH WOW (Highs)   Get married, Promoted, etc.

(Standard) Good

Bad

OH NO (Lows)

Death of Someone, loss of job, divorce, etc.

The Top Line is the "OH WOW" line. Anything from the "Good" line which is above "The Standard" line, up to this line, would measure positive events that happen in your life.

The Middle Line is the "Standard" line. This represents life as a regular day without any major events.

The Bottom Line, the "OH NO" line, represents the challenges that you face in your life. Anything from the "Bad" line down to this line measures everything negative that happens in your life.

If you have a tragic event, say a death in your family, you can see that this can drop you well below your life standard to the "OH NO" line. Likewise, if you have a major victory, like getting promoted, or getting engaged, you can be propelled up to the "OH WOW" line.

In life, we experience highs and lows. You are either moving forward and up or forward and down, but we don't move backwards. We simply choose to stay at certain levels depending on the circumstances that we encounter. Right now, you are probably saying, I'm not choosing to stay unhappy or mad, things have happened to me! Yes, things may have happened, but you must learn to adjust and choose to move on. This mindset becomes more relevant when facing a difficult challenge. We might become depressed, create a negative attitude, and feel that our life is meaningless. We might even feel that we are not even capable of moving forward. This is the point where we stop living and stay low on the chart. The thought of your life being worthless is simply not true, but this is how we get into trouble; we stop living for and trusting in God's plans.

You must remember that God is always with you and He wants you to focus on serving Him! You must also believe this and say this to yourself: All things are temporary; God is in control. During good times, we tend to recognize, rejoice and praise God when we are above the "standard" line. The challenge with this mindset is that you might get an unrealistic expectation of life and things might appear tougher when you fall again. Enjoy where you are, but understand the nature of the event that you are rejoicing in. Remember, ALL things in life are temporary, except for God.

When we fall below the standard line, this is when we start to doubt and question God. We might even become angry. When we get to this point, sometimes we tend to stay there and hold ourselves below life's standards. We might even feel like we have the right to stay down there. We don't.

We must learn to think and believe that everything happens for a reason. A great event is simply that; a great event. It isn't permanent or the new standard in your life. Likewise, a bad event is simply that; a bad event. Neither of them becomes the new standard in your life. You will only stay at a place that you choose to stay at, and you will only stay there if you choose to stay there.

Life's events do not happen to define us, they happen to "refine" us. We must keep moving forward and we must keep moving upwards.

"God allows us to go through challenges,
Not to DEFINE us, but to REFINE us."

Success

We often equate success with being happy. Please know that this isn't necessarily true. Your happiness is 100% dependent on you, not your circumstances or things. When you consider that "things" do not carry emotion; you can determine that your emotions about "things" are really a direct result of your own conscious or subconscious decisions. If you are an unhappy person, regardless of how successful you become, or how many things you buy, you are still you, so you will probably remain unhappy.

The questions to ask yourself are:

- How do I define success?
- How do I define happiness?
- How will I attain either one?

Success can and usually has different meanings to different people. It is important to find out what motivates you, what your goals are and what you were called to accomplish. You are your own unique person. God made you for and with a purpose. Sometimes situations that you are in can motivate you and can prompt you to become better. Success can and will have different meanings to different people. Some people measure success by money, others by fame and some by material possessions. However, those may not be the true measurements of success for you. If your goal is to be a better husband or wife and you have taken steps to make this happen and your family recognizes it, then you are indeed a success. If you choose to improve your life and your career, and you do, then you are successful.

Happiness

Happiness, on the other hand, is a state of mind, based on your reaction or response to something. Sometimes it might be a very difficult choice for you to be happy, especially if you are going through a hardship. Being sad and staying sad is a difficult mindset to come out of, so you must look inside of yourself, (not outside to things) to find and remember your own happiness. You can have many material things and personal relationships, but if you are not content with your own life, you will still not be happy.

Happiness is not offered by others, nor is it found in things. Buying a material possession or celebrating an event can certainly create joy, but true internal happiness is based on your decision to follow Christ. Appreciating where you are in life and what you have materialistically, is a big start. Understand that purchasing more items does not bring true happiness. You may not live or work where you want to and that's fine, but to move to the next level, you must learn to appreciate what you have today. God will provide blessings in your life in many ways, but how can He continue to bless you with more opportunity if you cannot appreciate where you already are and what you already have?

When you understand that every situation in your life is merely a steppingstone and part of God's plan, then you start to understand the value and importance of everything in your life. Everything that you do and every situation that you encounter, is a step that must be taken in order to get to the top of the next step. When you lose the importance of a life's step due to a setback, it will keep you from moving forward and moving closer towards God's plan for your life.

There is a purpose for your life.

We are born perfect in God's eyes, fully prepared to succeed, but along the way, we lose sight of whose we are and what we're capable of achieving through trusting in Him. Life happens to us and we start engaging in bad or unhealthy things. We might begin to abuse alcohol, drugs, food or something else. We might start getting angry, depressed, or create unhealthy addictions, thoughts or actions. Sometimes we completely redefine who we think we are, due to the confusion and deception in this world. However, God's message is very clear: He has already equipped you for His plan. You just need to trust in Him, accept Him and accept who He created you to be.

When you were born, do you remember that tag made of flesh attached to your side? You know, the one that said, "addict," "depressed," "anger issues," "fearful," "worried," "confused" or something else that was negative?

No, you say? You don't remember having that or even being born with an extra flesh tag with a negative description of yourself? Of course not, because it wasn't there.

The reason it wasn't there, is because God never put it there! This is the part where you might say, but Mike, I do have a defining negative characteristic and it is a part of me, but I've always been that way! This is where I tell you that you are wrong. God never gave you any negative defining characteristics. That was all your doing.

Living in a world dominated by sin, causes us to sin. Sometimes, we can sin so much and for so long that we can get confused and accept the sin as our own identity. We can confuse what we DO, as who we are. I challenge you to accept and believe that the things you DO, really aren't who you are. I'm not talking about shirking responsibility for your actions, I am talking about separating what God made you to be, versus what you have added to your life through what you DO. If you are doing things you shouldn't be doing, stop doing them! Once you stop doing those things, you will remove from your life what you brought in or introduced. God never intended those things to be there in the first place.

Sometimes, we do negative and sinful things for so long that we can cover ourselves in those things, hiding who we truly are. When diamonds are mined from the earth, the seekers can be deceived as they sort through thick chunks of carbon. However, if they can keep their eyes on the prize, not on the nasty carbon, the seekers can and usually will find the brilliant gems inside, covered by the years of darkness. It can be difficult to sort through thick layers of dark decay.

It requires great work to remove the layers of carbon to reveal the brilliance of the beautiful diamond inside.

Our lives with Christ are similar to mining diamonds.

God has given us His brilliant, shining light to be found inside, just like a brilliant and precious diamond is found embedded with layers of black, hardened carbon. The challenge is that some of us have hidden the brilliant light within, by covering ourselves with layers of dark carbon, represented by years of sinful nature, negative actions, and habits. Some of us have been sinning for so long that we have falsely accepted the layers of carbon as a part of who we are. When we do this, we allow the layers of darkness to prevent God's brilliant light within us from shining to the rest of the world, assuming we have accepted His light: Jesus.

The great news is that although you may not feel like you can remove the years of negativity or darkness that you may be trapped in, God loves you and He can! He makes all things new! He can help you remove the years of negative and sinful things that have been hiding His light inside of you if you only trust in Him!

Yes, you and God started your life journey and it will be just you and God who will end your life journey together, if you know Him. Will you be prepared to give an account of what you did according to His plans for your life?

You can be prepared…. right now.

Here is how:

The Bible says that the only way to know God is through Jesus. In fact, Jesus said, "I am the way, the truth, and the life. No one can come to the Father except through me." John 14: 6.

This means that by asking Jesus into your life, you can know God, be forgiven of your sins and have eternal life in Heaven. In your own words, pray and repent of your sins and confess that you believe Jesus died for your sins on the cross. Acknowledge Jesus Christ as your Lord and Savior and ask Him into your heart. Tell Him you want to start new.

If you said this prayer on your own free will right now, then congratulations, you have been saved and you are fully equipped to start a better plan, God's plan! Praise God.

However, you need to continue to do your part and live your life in a way that honors God, by getting into a Christian Church that teaches about Jesus and the Bible.

Now go forth and make your life exceptional!

- Mike Rodriguez

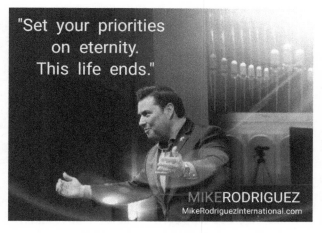

www.MikeRodriguezInternational.com

Chapter 1 – Your Life Is a Gift to You

Chapter 2

You Were Designed to Finish – Lessons from the Finish Line
By Pete Folch

Introduction – "This Is What You Trained For!"

December 7th, 2013 was a beautiful day for the annual Orlando half-marathon race! There were 19 runners representing my running/walking group for Discovery Church East Campus (Orlando), including 13 members running the 13.1-mile distance for the very first time! I remember many moments from the race. I was very proud of all my runners as they prepared well, and the goal was for everyone to finish their race. I ran with a group of runners and crossed the finish line step for step specifically with one of my runners. She was thrilled and exhausted at the same time! After getting some refreshments for her and making sure she was recovering OK, I handed my medal over to my wife. I ran back down the course to catch two other runners in my group. I checked on them, and I ended up pacing them to the finish line. Then I turned around to go back down course one more time to catch up with the last of the runners on my team. I sent her a text stating, "I am coming back to find you!" I wanted her to stay encouraged as she was on the course for a long time. When I found her, she appeared very relieved. As I paced with her, I kept reminding her of how close we were getting to the finish line! She was going to make it! The final turn in the Orlando Half-Marathon is down Rosiland Avenue (downtown Orlando), and the runners make a right turn onto Robinson Street. After you make the turn, you can see the finish line banner a few hundred yards ahead. At that moment I said, "Karyn, look ahead! There is the finish line! THIS IS WHAT YOU TRAINED FOR! With all the training you put in, you have earned this moment! As tired and exhausted as you are feeling, I want you to enjoy this moment. You are going to finish your first half-marathon!" What a beautiful and inspiring moment!

I have had the blessing of experiencing many finish-line moments like the one described above! God has inspired my heart to write a book titled: *"You Were Designed to Finish – Lessons from the Finish Line!"*

No, I'm not asking you to be a long-distance runner. I'm challenging you to be a "marathoner in your heart!" We get called to various long-distance journeys in our lives. The journeys can be physical, business, educational, career, financial, family/relational, ministry, and ultimately our legacy finish lines. A legacy finish line is staying faithful to living out God's call on our lives to make a difference for Christ all the way to the end of our lives. As we reach the end of our lives, I believe God wants us to be able to make the claim like the Apostle Paul, in 2 Timothy 4:7 *"For I have fought the good fight, I have finished the race, I have kept the faith."*

In this chapter, I will share eight lessons I have learned about pursuing the finish line. I'm sharing from my experience with long-distance running since 1981 when I ran my first marathon as a junior in college. Prior to college, I was not a runner. I actually hated running. I am not a physically gifted runner at 6'3" and weighing 200+ pounds. But God has changed my life in many ways since I came to faith in Christ in October of 1979 during my freshman year. I am sharing from a background of having run 23 marathon events and five ultra-marathons. My longest ultra-marathon was 100 kilometers (62 miles) in 2013. I have also competed in 3 Olympic distance triathlons, and one 200-mile RAGNAR relay run in Washington, DC. Much greater than all these individual finish line achievements, to date, is that I've coached 42 other people to run and complete their first half or full distance marathon. I have experienced a lot of finish line moments! Enjoy the following insights and lessons from the finish line!

1 – Everyone Needs a High-Five!

Proverbs 18:21 "For the power of life and death is in the tongue."

In January 2019, I was at the Walt Disney World Marathon in Orlando. I ran in five of the past six Walt Disney World Marathon races, but this year I was a spectator, tracking three runners in the race. My first strategically planned spot to catch my runners was near mile marker #4. I stood right along the barrier fence shouting out words of encouragement to all runners going by as I was specifically trying to spot my runners. As a distance runner, I always appreciate the shouts and cheers of encouragement. As I yelled out encouragement, I held my left hand out to offer a "high five" to any runner who was going by. I was blown away by how many runners made a special effort to come by and touch my hand. Some runners would speed up or slow down to work their way over to the side fence railing where I was. I wondered if maybe I was creating a safety hazard by holding my hand out to offer a high five. I touched the hands with people I did not know from different countries. I touched hundreds of hands of people I had never met before and will likely never meet again. My left hand had a high concentration of other people's perspiration (Yes, I did have hand sanitizer with me). I saw so many folks go out of their way to receive a high five.

Now, not everyone came over to receive a "high five." Not everyone wanted to touch my hand. For many, simply hearing cheers of encouragement was good enough for them. When I say everyone needs a "high five," what I mean is people need some form of encouragement! For many, encouragement is words of praise or affirmation! "Way to go! Keep it up! You are doing great! Keep running strong!" For others, encouragement could be a physical high-five, fist bump, applause, a thumbs up, quietly being there for someone or a physical note. Encouragement is the squeeze of a hand and even a warm hug!

Chapter 2 – You Were Designed to Finish- Lessons from the Finish Line

Part of how I help coach people to complete these races is through sharing words of encouragement! I have run or walked with hundreds of people over a 37-year period of running long distances. When we finish a training run, as appropriate there are high fives, there are fist bumps, and even applause. Not everyone is comfortable hugging, especially if they are all sweaty. Support and encouragement are different for different people. Everyone has different variations in their "encouragement language." However, the need for encouragement never grows old! One of my favorite quotes from Zig Ziglar is: "A lot of people have gone further than they thought they could because somebody else thought they could!"

Your words of encouragement can provide the spark to keep someone from giving up. Your positive gesture can send the message "I support you," and can positively change the direction of their day, and maybe their life. Even your presence can make a difference! As a runner, I have run some races in very bad weather; I appreciate the people who came out in bad weather to still support us. Their presence means a lot and is encouraging.

Yes, people are encouraged in different ways (as not every runner needed a high five touch at mile 4). However, EVERYONE NEEDS ENCOURAGEMENT. There is a world out there starving for encouragement! Ask God to help you be an instrument of encouragement to others around you! As is referenced in Proverbs 18:21, be the person who speaks those "words of life" to others!

"High-five" people with your words!

"High-five" people with your life!

2 – Together Has Power

Hebrews 10:24-25a "And let us consider how we may spur one another on toward love and good deeds, not giving up meeting together, as some are in the habit of doing, but encouraging one another."

I continue to hear testimonies over the last eight years from my runners and walkers in the DCE Running and Walking group where they have noticed such a difference between running/walking with the group versus going by themselves. Here are some of the comments:

- "Today, I ran/walked so much stronger!"
- "Today, I did not realize I was running that fast!"
- "Today, I went farther than I thought I could go!"
- "Today, it did not feel as hard!"
- "Today, the time flew by for our training run!"
- "Today, I felt smoother in this training run!"
- "Today, my recovery was so much better!"

These comments validate the power of the team, the power of support, the power of fellowship, the power of the group, the power of being with others going the same direction you are. We are so much stronger together than alone! We were never meant to go through our journey alone as followers of Christ! "Together Has Power" is the theme of our running group. A few years ago, we had shirts made with the "Together Has Power" theme printed on them. When we started our group in 2011, the inspiration came from the "Together Has Power" video story of Rick and Dick Hoyt. The video is about a father and son who have done over 1000 races together despite the son (Rick) having cerebral palsy. The 4 ½ minute video ends with "Together Has Power – Don't Run Alone!"

In 37 years of training for marathons, I have completed many long training runs by myself. Not a lot of people want to join you at 5:00 a.m. to run 18 miles. I get it. However, running or walking is a lot more enjoyable when we do the miles together! The team is a lot safer and healthier running or walking with others, not to mention the fellowship and bonding that takes place. I do not want anyone running or walking alone. For our run/walk group events, I try to find someone for everyone to pace with. If I cannot find someone to pace with a runner or walker, I will pace with that individual.

Are you trying to go at it alone? Whatever your goal, your endeavor, your journey, your mission, or your God-given calling, are you trying to do it all by yourself? Are you connected or in a situation where you are able to help others, and they are able to help you? Hebrews 10:24-25 says, *"And let us consider how we may spur one another on toward love and good deeds, not giving up meeting together, as some are in the habit of doing, but encouraging one another—and all the more as you see the day approaching."*

Communication and psychology experts generally agree that today, we are more "electronically or digitally" connected than ever before. Yet today, there are more people than ever before feeling lonely and relationally distant from each other. God did not design us to be soloists with no human contact. These words are not meant to guilt anyone to start going to church, join a small group Bible Study, join a club, participate in a business network, or enroll in a mastermind group. However, I am convinced that none of us can become the best version of ourselves without help from others and vice versa! No one I know has made it to the finish line without help from others along the way! "Together Has Power" is not simply a positive phrase, but it is a healthy way to operate in your life!

3 – The Character of Perseverance

James 1:2-4 "Consider it pure joy, my brothers and sisters, whenever you face trials of many kinds, because you know that the testing of your faith produces perseverance. Let perseverance finish its work so that you may be mature and complete, not lacking anything."

After all these years of running marathons, ultra-marathons, and other unique distance challenges, I often get asked the question: "How much of finishing a marathon is 'physical,' and how much is 'mental'?" Answering from my own experience, I would rate training for and finishing a marathon as 30% "physical" and 70% "mental." Absolutely no question about it, you have to get the proper physical training in. You have to get those training miles deposited into your "running bank account" to be ready for race day. However, there is a much stronger mental component factoring into staying with your program and finishing your race.

In the dictionary, "perseverance" is persistence in doing something despite the difficulty. Perseverance is the resolve and the courage to stay in the battle during challenging situations. I inform first-time runners to know what is coming ahead: "You are going to get tested and challenged." I want them to be prepared and ready. In most any long-distance journey, you are going to get tested and challenged! You must be willing to go through the challenge and resolve not to give up. From the Bible, James 1:3 says, *"Because you know that the testing of your faith produces perseverance."* So for us to develop the character of perseverance, we have to be challenged. We have to feel the pressure. We don't learn or grow very much when things are always easy! When we are stretched and face difficulties, we grow.

Perseverance, mental strength, toughness, "grit" is not necessarily found in the person with the greatest physical strength. Perseverance is found in the cancer patient with a weakened body determined to fight off the illness. Perseverance is found in the person who continues looking for a job and refuses to get discouraged after being turned down 20+ times in their job search. Perseverance is found in the individual who has failed multiple times to pass the state certification exam but continues to study and prepare for the next opportunity afforded him or her. Perseverance is found in the spouse who remains faithful after a mentally debilitating disease causes life-long non-stop care of their spouse. Perseverance is found in the person who keeps praying daily for 30+ years for a family member to receive Christ! In the movie "Rocky Balboa" (2006) Rocky defined perseverance with his son: *"It's not about how hard you hit. It's about how hard you can get hit and keep moving forward. How much you can take and keep moving forward."*

My daughter, Tessa, in her first year as a head coach for middle school volleyball players asked me, "Dad, how do you teach grit? How do you teach mental toughness?" I responded, "You can only talk so much about mental toughness. As a coach, teacher, mentor, influencer, you have to model grit! Some things are more effectively caught than taught!" People need to see perseverance modeled in your life. James 1:2 says to *"Consider it pure joy, my brothers and sisters, whenever you encounter trials of many kinds because you know that the testing of your faith produces endurance."* Rather than trying to escape the challenge God has for us, we need to embrace challenges as opportunities to grow and believe God will bring us through it!

Perseverance is learned in the marathon/ultramarathon journey as well as in many other of life's journey and challenges. James 1:4 says, *"Let perseverance finish its work so that you may be mature and complete, not lacking anything."* I am not a theologian or Bible scholar, but I believe James 1:4 is saying: The more perseverance is developed in us, the more mature we are in our character!

4 – Give God Your Best

Colossians 3:23 "Whatever you do, work at it with all your heart, as working for the Lord,"

Chapter 2 – You Were Designed to Finish-
Lessons from the Finish Line

I've been asked: "After all of these marathons and ultra-marathons you've done, does it ever get to be routine?" My answer to the question is, "NO! ...absolutely NO! Marathon running NEVER gets routine!" I do not ever take a marathon for granted nor do I take the marathon training program for granted.

First of all, no two marathons or ultra-marathon races are ever the same! Marathon training is never the same. I've completed a training program and remained completely healthy, not missing a training run at all. I've gone through a training program and have had to battle through illness and/or battle through an injury causing me to miss some weeks of training. I've gone through some marathon training programs where I have had to deal with a heavy travel schedule and bad weather causing me to alter the training. When it comes to race day, I've experienced pretty much every type of race condition: freezing temperatures, temperatures as high at 87 degrees (for a 100K race!), wind, rain, fog, humidity, bright sunshine, darkness of night, bunched together with thousands, running alone for miles, and every kind of race surface, sidewalk, bridge, or trail. I've run the same event for multiple years and had different experiences. The variability of the marathon is the way it is with life. You have to be ready and adapt to what comes at you. Each day of our lives can come with new surprises... it is never routine. Do not take life for granted!

Second, the moment I back off and treat a marathon as "routine" I am in trouble of not being prepared and at risk of not finishing the race! There is nothing routine about running a marathon. A lot can happen over the course of

26.2 miles or longer. The marathon event involves the physical body and managing the mind. My body has changed, and it is not the same as when I was running in my 20's. I notice stretching and warming up takes longer. I notice recovery sometimes takes me longer. I notice my body can be more sensitive to changes of shoes, running alignment, and other "little things." It is so important to keep the momentum and rhythm. The same is true with keeping up positive habits and our spiritual disciplines like Bible reading, praying, fellowship, or spending quiet time with God. If we back off or take the approach that we can skip on these practices, we will put ourselves in the position of losing our rhythm and being unprepared to handle life.

Thirdly and most importantly, I want to honor God with my effort! I will train for each marathon like it's my first marathon. I want to give the best I have. Colossians 3:23 *"Whatever you do, work at it with all your heart, as working for the Lord."* I realize I am extremely blessed to be running these marathons and ultra-marathons over a 37+ year time frame. Part of my expression of praise to God is using the gifts, talents, blessings, and strength He has given me to honor Him. My gratitude for the ability to run these long distances is expressed by training well and running to the best of my ability and training other first-time runners to the best of my ability! Every one of us has been blessed with gifts, talents, and abilities, and we honor God with how we use them. In my career and out in the marketplace, I have heard the question, "How can I make an impact for Christ at work?" Be excellent at what you are called to do! We do not want to treat each day of our lives as routine. Each day is a gift from

God, for us to use what He has given us to His glory. Give God the best you have every day.

5 – Miracles Do Happen

Isaiah 40:31 *"but those who hope in the LORD will renew their strength. They will soar on wings like eagles; they will run and not grow weary, they will walk and not be faint."*

I've experienced first-hand the truth: God is about restoration, making things new again, bringing new life and strength physically, mentally, emotionally, and spiritually! I have run about 22,000 miles, and I have experienced a lot of aches, soreness, and pains. Sometimes the pain is due to having a good, strong, hard workout, so it is a healthy soreness. I've experienced some "overuse" related injuries due to running/training more than I should or stepping up the training too quickly. I've also had injuries due to pushing shoes too far. The following are two types of discomfort or pain I experienced that led to a miracle.

BLOOD CLOTS

In March 2014, I was experiencing a very strong running season because I was feeling good after my workouts and recovering well. I've always been good about stretching. Later in the month, I started to have trouble stretching out my left calf muscle. I would run, and the calf muscle felt very tight, almost like I had a cramp, which is very weird. On March 26, 2014, I went to see a doctor about a different issue, and he happened to notice my left leg in the exam room, which was a God thing! He said, "Your lower left leg looks so big." My response was, "The left calf muscle has always been a little bit bigger than my right because my left leg is the "drive leg" to do lay-ups (and slam dunks) when I played basketball." He said he thought there was more going on and he said, "I think you have a blood clot." He immediately ordered an ultrasound test, and they found two blood clots. Upon finding the two blood clots, I was ordered to remain at the hospital as this condition can be life-threatening if the clots break off and travel to the heart and lungs.

Here I am, a disciplined, active runner with two blood clots in the leg. To this day, they do not know what caused those clots. I was put on a daily prescription of Xarelto (powerful blood thinner). Thankfully, I did not experience side effects from taking Xarelto. I was thankful for the prayers of so many in my group and church. Eventually, I was cleared to go home and slowly get back into running. My calf muscle felt much better, but my quarterly check-ups showed there were still issues with clots and coagulation. They told me I would probably have to be taking Xarelto for the rest of my life. I don't like taking any pills, and Xarelto is very expensive. Many folks were praying for the clots to completely clear. To add to the mix, my current health insurance coverage was ending soon (that is another story) which would make my out-of-pocket costs even higher for the Xarelto. A year and a half later, I was getting my final ultrasound before my current coverage expired and I was given the "ALL CLEAR!" What a sweeping turn of events! No more blood clots or coagulation issues, and no more having to take Xarelto. Miracle! Thank you, Lord!

KNEE MENISCUS TEAR

In March 2017, I started to feel some pain in my left knee upon running or any kind of movement. I know my body pretty well; however, I had not felt this type of knee pain before. I could not bend the knee very well without distinctive pain. In April, I finished a 5K and was in great pain. I was grimacing as I walked. As I taught my workshops and seminars, I would feel discomfort moving around the classroom. I tried resting and slowing down my pace. I visited a sports medicine clinic, and they gave me some exercises to try in order to strengthen my knee. They also told me if the pain I was feeling was a "3" on a scale of 1 - 10, I could run and not exacerbate the injury. I still felt pain throughout the summer, and my runners noticed the definite limp I had.

Begrudgingly in August 2017, I decided to get an MRI exam on my left knee. The MRI revealed a significant tear of the medial meniscus. The doctor said, "You are going to have to get surgery to get it repaired. There is no blood flow to the meniscus, so there is no way it will heal itself." They said the surgery would be a quick procedure where they will clip the portion that is torn, and after rehabilitation/therapy I should be able to run again in about 4-6 weeks. They also mentioned with this type of surgery, I would be more prone to arthritis in the knee and blood clotting, IN MY LEFT LEG! Given my history, they were going to put me on medication after the surgery! "No," I thought, "this can't be happening!"

I went through the process of verifying coverage for the surgery in September of 2017, planning for the post-surgery, and scheduling of therapy visits. I continued to pray and ask God for wisdom. I was blessed to have a certified athletic trainer and a medical doctor join our run group. I consulted with them on what they had seen with meniscus injuries. My athletic trainer friend had seen cross country runners with meniscus tears wait until after the season to have surgery. After consulting with them and continued prayer, I decided to cancel the surgery just one week before the surgery was supposed to happen! I opted to try to manage through the injury. I trained for the 2018 Disney Marathon training at a pace of 2 minutes per mile slower than my normal to manage the pain. I still was able to work with a brand-new runner to help him train for his first marathon. We ran the 2018 Disney marathon step for step, and what a thrill finishing with him was! However, I was still feeling the pain. One of the other marathoners told me, "OK Pete, it is now time to get the surgery!"

In December 2017, I got news; my name was drawn for the 2018 Chicago Marathon lottery. So I had another marathon coming in October of 2018. Our official training would begin in the summer. I tried to continue with managing the meniscus injury. My prayer was, "Lord, I want to be able to pace with the other marathoners who are also preparing for Chicago!" The goal: to manage the pain and somehow progress back to my previous pace and be able to train together with my other runners. God gave me an incredible and extraordinary summer of training; I was able to keep pace with the other runners and the flexibility in my left knee dramatically improved! I ran the Chicago marathon 37 minutes faster than the Disney race nine months earlier. Three weeks later, I finished a 32-mile ultra-marathon race in Deerfield Beach, FL in 84-degree weather! "My left knee has been healed!" I thought, "No surgery needed! Thank you, Lord, for the miracle!!"

By no means am I promoting going against a doctor's recommendation! I will clearly state that I believe God heals through the skills of a doctor, through specific medical procedures, and through appropriate medicine. I also believe God heals supernaturally today in 2019. Do your homework and seek good counsel (maybe 2nd and 3rd opinions) and be tuned to the Holy Spirit. Somehow I sensed God saying to wait, to be patient, to endure the discomfort (OK, the pain!), and that HE is going to orchestrate an extraordinary outcome in HIS timing. Isaiah 40:31 *"but those who hope in the LORD will renew their strength. They will soar on wings like eagles; they will run and not grow weary, they will walk and not be faint."* God does miracles! He can bring new strength in your body, in your relationships, in your family, in your marriage, in your career, in your vitality, in your emotions, in your spirit, in your (you fill in the blank) _____. There is not any situation He cannot repair and restore!

6 - Bring Others to the Finish Line

Acts 20:24 – *"However, I consider my life worth nothing to me; my only aim is to finish the race and complete the task the Lord Jesus has given me—the task of testifying to the good news of God's grace."*

Some have asked, "What has been your greatest race?" The greatest marathon race experience for me is the 1996 Boston Marathon. I had the chance to run the 100th Anniversary Boston Marathon in 1996, and the race was a very special and unique experience. For ultra-marathons, my greatest race is the 2013 Palm 100 (100-kilometer race). Palm 100 is the only time I have run 62 miles in a race!

However, if someone asked me, "What is my great running achievement?" Unequivocally, the answer is helping and coaching *(as of this writing)* 42 other runners to successfully run their first half or full distance marathon! What a blessing to be involved in helping someone else get to the finish line. I don't mean coaching or giving advice from a distance, but to run and train right alongside these runners! Then, ultimately, for a number of my runners, to run the actual race with them, which has been amazing! There have been some emotional "finish line" moments for both me and my fellow runners. To hear comments like, "I can't believe I did this! I ran my first half-marathon... I finished a marathon!" is extraordinary! There is a joy for me to see those finisher medals draped around the necks of my runners. Oh yes, (keeping it real here) there have been a few folks in those post-finish-line moments, with their body feeling the peak of exhaustion and/or pain of what they just went through, may say something like "Yes, I finished! ...but I am never going to do this again." Two days later many of those folks are talking about training for another race, and that is pretty normal. I remember telling one of my runners who finished her first and only marathon at Disney World: "You are a marathon finisher! You are a Disney World Marathon Finisher! And you will have that title for the rest of your life!"

God has called all of us to be "finishers!" I also believe God has called all of us to help others in their journey to be "finishers." We all have a role in helping others discover the hope, the redemption, the salvation, the "true life" which comes from placing our faith in Christ. The Apostle Paul states the point well in Acts 20:24, *"However, I consider my life worth nothing to me; my only aim is to finish the race and complete the task the Lord Jesus has given me—the task of testifying to the good news of God's grace."* For Paul to finish well meant bringing others to faith in Jesus Christ, including all the way to the end of his life on earth! In a marathon, (except for the few world-class elite runners) most everyone is not competing against another runner. The ultimate goal is to finish and to finish strong by keeping the faith and sharing it with others! There are some runners trying to finish under a goal time or make a qualifying time. However, 98% of the runners are not directly competing against someone else. Each runner can achieve their goal running in the same race. We can help others successfully get to the finish line!

I think the finish line is a little bit of what heaven will be like. You have all of these runners coming in at different times into the finish line area, completing their journey and receiving their finisher medal. In Hebrews 12:1, it says, *"Let us run our race with perseverance, the race marked out before us..."*

Scripture validates that everyone has a "race" we are called to run! The "race marked out" is God's specific calling on our lives. Later, verse two says to *"fix our eyes on Jesus."* It is about keeping Christ the focus and at the center; fixing our eyes on Jesus and not ourselves. For those who follow Christ, there is going to be a great celebration crossing the finish line as we pass on from our earthly life into heaven. Let's do everything we can to help everyone get to the finish line, finishing well, finishing strong!

7 – Integrity of Your Commitment

1 Corinthians 9:24, 26a *"In a race everyone runs, but only one person gets first prize. So run your race to win. So I run straight to the goal with purpose in every step."*

The accomplishment of completing a marathon is hard to fake. Either you completed the distance, or you didn't. A person who isn't active and has a very sedentary lifestyle cannot just decide to run their first marathon tomorrow without any training; it would be a foolish attempt. You have to put in the training. You have to get the miles in. In all my years of running, I only know of one "first-time marathoner" who did not do any road-running and ran his first marathon. The "first-timer" was a friend of mine from Tampa, and he played on a premier state champion rugby team. He was very physically fit from being an active rugby player, and so he had the cardio-vascular fitness from doing plenty of running up and down the field. He definitely was not inactive or sedentary. He also had the mental courage and toughness, which also comes from rugby and all those scrums.

I get nervous when I see a few videos people post on YouTube saying they didn't do much training for the Disney Marathon and they finished. These stories are a few exceptions! You do not see videos made by those who didn't finish! The reality is there are consequences when you approach the marathon start-line unprepared. I like to emphasize with "first-time marathoners" DO NOT CUT SHORT YOUR TRAINING PROGRAM. As you go through the weeks of a marathon training program, you are putting miles in your "running bank account." The marathon day is when you withdraw on those training miles! There is a danger to thinking you can shortcut your training. If you come to the start-line of a marathon unprepared to run 26.2 miles, you risk the following:

- not finishing the race
- getting hurt or injured
- having a higher risk of "hitting the wall" (physiological-mental breakdown)
- getting taken off the course if you cannot hold pace (most marathons have a 6-hour finish time limit. Disney is an exception with a 7-hour time limit)
- finish, but your recovery will be much longer and more painful
- sustain a more permanent injury, shortcutting your abilities to run again

Chapter 2 – You Were Designed to Finish-
Lessons from the Finish Line

Most marathon training programs are designed to gradually get your mileage up safely with the proper recovery and rest. These training programs are designed so if you follow the program, you will be more than ready to complete the distance. Even if conditions are not so favorable or you are not having your best day, YOU ARE STILL PREPARED TO FINISH THE DISTANCE! You will be more confident knowing you did your preparation!

Along with the risks and safety issues described above, I feel there is "integrity" with the commitment to train for a marathon. Count the cost before making the commitment! Before I make the commitment to the race, I talk to my beautiful wife Lisa as she understands what the commitment means to train for the long races. She has been such a patient, gracious, faithful support to me! I review the schedule. I review other family commitments. I review the time of year I will be training for 16 weeks. I review the race. I review "my heart" and motivation. I review if we have some "first-time marathoners" getting ready. I review the financial impact. MOST IMPORTANTLY, I PRAY! Whether a marathon training program or a life journey, stay true to your commitment! (Matthew 5:37) Do not try to shortcut the program! A football coach from high school reminded me: *"The desire to win is useless without the desire to prepare!"* The preparation matters! Your integrity matters! Have the willingness to prepare! In 1 Corinthians 9:24, Paul wants us to RUN YOUR RACE TO WIN (TLB). Keep the integrity of following Christ and realize you are to live every day in your "call." Be true to live a life honoring and reflecting HIM faithfully, bringing HIS message of Hope.

Through your life and sometimes your words, preach the gospel message to the world; RUNNING YOUR RACE TO WIN!

8 - Pace Your Race

Hebrews 12: 1-2a *"Therefore, since we are surrounded by such a great cloud of witnesses, let us throw off everything that hinders and the sin that so easily entangles. And let us run with perseverance the race marked out for us, fixing our eyes on Jesus, the pioneer, and perfecter of faith."*

Every one of us is on a journey! Every one of us is running a race, which is ultimately our calling marked out by God. One of the big keys to finishing your race is to pace yourself. Sometimes, going out too hard and too fast can get you hurt, create discouragement, and get you burned out. Hebrews 12:2 does not say "Let us run with speed!" The Scripture does not say "sprint your way." The verse does say (in six different Bible translations below):

- *"let us run with perseverance the race marked out for us,"* (NIV)
- *"let us run with endurance the race that is set before us,"* (NASB)
- *"let us run with patience the race that is set before us,"* (KJV)
- *"let us run with patience the particular race that God has set before us."* (TLB)
- *"let us run with endurance and active persistence the race that is set before us* (AMP)

- *"run life's marathon race with passion and determination, for
  the path has been already marked out before us. (TPT)*

Patience is defined as endurance under difficult
circumstances. Life's journey will also have different
challenges along the way. We must exercise patience and not
try to rush the result. Building a relationship takes time.
Proper healing from an injury takes time. Training a brand-
new manager takes time. Searching for a new key leader for
your organization takes time. Building the culture of an
organization takes time. Building customer loyalty and
goodwill for a business takes time.

When a couple gets married, there can be such an
emphasis placed on the wedding day! Yes, the wedding day
is a significant day. However, if one is not careful, there can
be too much energy and preparation placed on the wedding
day. It's the big Day 1 of the marriage. But what about Day
2? ...or Day 3?...Day 4?...Day 28?...or Day 64? What about
preparing to pace ourselves for a lifetime of being married?
Pace the race!

When we take on a "sprinters" mentality, we are
more likely to quit when things get difficult. No disrespect
to sprinters, but sprinting is for short races. Finishing the
long race requires pace! We live in a world which wants
instant results for everything. Yes, there are times where the
quick and immediate is necessary for the situation. However,
in most situations, pacing yourself in the journey means you
will run stronger! You are less prone to quitting.

Chapter 2 – You Were Designed to Finish-
Lessons from the Finish Line

The goal is to get to the finish line successfully. You probably have heard the famous quote, *"slow and steady wins the race."* The phrase is associated with Aesop's fable of "The Tortoise and the Hare." The meaning is, "If you work slowly but constantly, you will succeed better than if you work fast for a short while and do not continue." God is not as concerned about how fast we are traveling but concerned that we stay in the race! Approach your race with patience, endurance, and perseverance! Pace your race!

Conclusion – "My Power Is Made Perfect in Weakness"

2 Corinthians 12:9a *"But he said to me, 'My grace is sufficient for you, for my power is made perfect in weakness.'"*

In my high school Physical Education class, we had the 600-yard run/walk test, and I feared having to run the distance. I started to get into running in my college years when I tried to do something to keep in shape since I wasn't playing varsity sports.

The summer of 1981, a good friend gave me the book, "I'm Running to Win" by Ann Kiemel. The book was the story of her faith journey, which took a non-athletic woman and propelled her into finishing her first marathon and eventually qualifying for the great Boston Marathon. After reading the book, I was inspired to train for my first marathon at the age of 19. I completed my first marathon in October of 1981 ("City of Lakes" Marathon in Minneapolis, MN) finishing in about four hours. I remember two weeks prior to the marathon, I came down with a very bad sinus infection. The infection really sapped my strength. I kept wondering, "OK God, will I have enough strength to complete my first attempt at 26.2 miles?" I ran the race with a handkerchief affixed to the side of my shorts! After I finished, and after all the congratulations, hugs, greetings, and celebrations, my mother said, "You no longer sound congested."

When you train for the marathon, you are going to get tested and challenged. When you train to develop yourself to be a stronger Christian, you are going to get tested. There are going to be trials in the journey! The Apostle Paul says in 2 Corinthians 12:9-10 *"But he said to me, 'My grace is sufficient for you, for my power is made perfect in weakness.' Therefore, I will boast all the more gladly about my weaknesses, so that Christ's power may rest on me. That is why, for Christ's sake, I delight in weaknesses, in insults, in hardships, in persecutions, in difficulties. For when I am weak, then I am strong."*

God will allow us to be in positions and situations where the only way we succeed is depending on Him and His powerful intervention; having His Power working in our weakness. In addition to the miraculous interventions mentioned in Lesson 5, here are three more from my marathon experience, highlighting His Power working in my weakness!

1) In 1994, I was training for the inaugural Walt Disney World Marathon, and the training was going very strong. The week before that marathon, I was on a simple taper run, and I severely sprained my ankle. I couldn't walk for the next four days, and the situation

certainly looked like no chance of the ankle healing quick enough to run 26.2 miles in a few days. Two days before the marathon (with a heavy bandage) I could put weight on my right foot. The day before the marathon, I was able to run a couple of miles (my first time since the injury). The day of the marathon, I ran and finished the 1st Walt Disney World Marathon. God says, "My power is perfected in weakness."

2) I've always battled through ankle injuries with my sports career. In 2007, as I was getting treatment for Iliotibial Band Syndrome, an X-ray examination revealed a big buildup of scar tissue in my right ankle causing the ankle not to heal properly. I was told surgery was needed to correct my "crooked" right ankle issue, or I might be prone to foot and ankle issues for the rest of my life, and I may not be able to run much longer. Well as of 2019, I am still running strong on the "crooked" right ankle with no issue. God says, "My power is perfected in weakness."

3) In March 2013, I was preparing to take on the longest distance race of my life, the Palm100 Ultra-Marathon! The distance was 100 kilometers, which translates to 62 miles (or running about 2 ½ marathons!). Weeks prior to the race, I was praying for cool weather and constantly tracking the long-

range weather trends. High heat is the worst challenge for distance runners. The day of the race the temperature got up to 87 degrees with high humidity and stayed at that temperature for about 10 hours (hottest ultra-marathon on record for Palm100)! Other races have been canceled when the heat gets this high! I did everything I could to try to manage the heat. Ultimately God brought me through these horrible conditions. Then in the heat of the Palm100, He used me to help a runner who was about to quit at mile 19 as he was suffering from "lactic acid syndrome" in his legs. We ran together for the next 43 miles challenging, pushing, and encouraging each other, and we finished together! (1 Thessalonians 5:11) Is that not God?! God says, "MY POWER IS PERFECTED IN WEAKNESS!"

You were designed to finish! Some powerful life lessons come from the journey on our way to the finish line. God is calling for all of us to get to the finish line! HE will get us there! HE will help you and I finish strong!

About the Author – Pete Folch

**Speaker/Trainer
Founder/President of
Second Wind-Finish
Strong, Inc.**

Pete Folch is a professional keynote speaker and accomplished trainer dedicated to teaching, serving, inspiring and motivating people and teams, to achieve peak performance and significance in their lives. Pete has a passion to help people discover renewed energy and re-discover their true potential …..and ultimately finish strong in their "race of life." Pete lives in Orlando, FL.

Pete is one of the original members of the founding class of Ziglar Legacy Certified Trainers. As a professional contract trainer, Pete has conducted workshops all over the U.S. Pete receives frequent invitations from clients he serves to come back and present again!

Married 30+ years, Pete and his beautiful wife have two outstanding young adult children. During his 34-year restaurant career, his greatest accomplishment: Revitalizing team energy and transforming the culture for 55,000+ employees in over 400 Olive Garden restaurants in the U.S. & Canada. Pete is also a Darden "Brilliance Award" recipient (the top Darden honor). Pete has:

- Served as the Mental Strength and Conditioning Coach for the Florida Flight semi-pro basketball team.
- Run 23 marathons, including the Boston Marathon! He completed the ultra-marathon distances of 50 kilometers, 50 miles and 100 kilometers!
- Coached and trained 42 runners (with little running background) to successful completion of their first half or full distance marathon!
- Been the voice of "Rev Radio," a professional motivational series of presentations for his past employer, Darden.
- Served as the enthusiastic PA announcer for the Florida Flight semi-pro team …and has even called games at the Orlando Amway Center (Home of the NBA's Orlando Magic).
- Received the 2011 Central Florida FCA "Servant Leader Award."
- Presented at 270+ seminars/corporate events in 2016 and 2017! Among 300+ contract trainers at Pryor Learning, he earned Top Ten Finalist in 2016 & 2017 in multiple performance categories including Highest Customer Satisfaction!
- International experience with teaching and presenting in Italy and Canada.

With a focus on "Redefining the Possible," Pete has tangibly helped hospitality and service organizations achieve record setting business results. With high integrity and excellent service, he has trained and coached professionals in food service, health care, real estate, technology, education, coaching/consulting, church ministry, contractors, fitness/wellness, law enforcement, government and the military...as well as college/high school students.

Pete's most popular keynote messages or programs:

"Keys to Personal Revitalization,"
"Running Your Race on a Crooked Ankle,"
"Keys to Getting to Your Finish Line,"
"Leading with Impact,"
"Goal Setting and Achievement" and
"A Passion for Service-Connecting Everyone with Your Mission!"

Pete Folch - Founder/President
Second Wind - Finish Strong, Inc.
Transformational Training - Revitalization Consulting

www.secondwindfinishstrong.com

Contact:
peterfolchjr@gmail.com

You've Got a "Second Wind" in You!

Chapter 2 – You Were Designed to Finish-
Lessons from the Finish Line

Chapter 3

Preparing for Purpose
By Velma Knowles

A one-on-one meeting with your manager... We've all had them in our professional lives, and even in our personal ones. Such meetings can be any or all of usually three things: opportunities, challenges, or learning moments. A chance to tout your accomplishments, a way to stretch your current abilities, or a time to listen and absorb an objective assessment of your performance.

My manager – let's call him Paul – scheduled one such encounter I will never forget. One that changed my life's course forever.

I had sat in prior meetings with Paul and seldom found them to be comfortable, more often quite challenging. You know how someone can "rub you the wrong way?" You feel like you are oil and they are water? Or maybe you feel like they are the sandpaper and you are the wood. That is exactly how it was when Paul entered the picture. I remember the first time I met with him for an introductory meeting. I was well along in my career. Paul became my manager. We sat around a big round table in what was, at that time, my office.

At that initial meeting, he asked me about my role. My instincts immediately told me he was questioning my value. He asked, "Are you really making a difference? Are you making an impact on the department, the organization?" There was a lesson God was about to teach me.

The lesson: My pride was too big, and my insecurities were on full display. I was trusting more in my own strength and not God's. Of course, I was a Christian; I knew the Lord and, what I now realize, is that God was in His own way preparing me for my purpose. So, for our next one-on-one months later, I scooped up the folder of notes I thought I might need, threw my shoulders back, and entered the conference room smiling and coming across as brimming with confidence. Paul was seated at one end of an oval table that was normally surrounded by twelve people. Here, though, it was just the two of us. He was flipping through a folder of his own. He looked stern and full of serious business, so I sat at the other end of the table.

He looked up, peered over his glasses, and opened with, "Velma Knowles." Right then, even as a relative novice on the continuum of leadership, I knew this was not going to go well for me. How was I going to handle this moment? Which door would I choose? Would this be an opportunity, a challenge, or a learning moment? I selected door number three, a learning moment, or rather, door number three selected me. I had sensed from previous hallway meetings with him and other colleagues that he was frustrated with me and the way I handled work situations. It was the type of serious tone and mode of address that we often experienced from our parents as children when we got in trouble. The use of a full name from a superior was a full stop sign. You had to pay attention. Stop. And listen.

I remember Paul peering at me and calling me a "knucklehead." Then proceeding to run through a laundry list of my shortcomings as a leader. He had specific dates and examples of each of my failings.

"You play favorites."

"You micro-manage your people."

"You waffle from one day to the other."

"You're inconsistent."

"You don't understand the business."

"You forget who's running the show here."

On and on he went. "The world does not revolve around you, Velma Knowles." I was this, I was that. The apparent blatant criticism flowed. I closed my folder and stared vacantly at him, dumbfounded, forlorn, and helpless. It was the longest and most painful 20 minutes of my now apparently worthless professional life.

I had nothing to say, no defense because I had not prepared for this. I was totally blindsided. I couldn't see how my own failures had brought me to this crossroad. At that moment, I felt so abused. I was angry at how someone could treat me with such disrespect. Each day after I felt less and less valued, as my own perceived value diminished until it was next to zero. At that time, I defined my worth based on my job, title, and my role. Maybe you are thinking that way now. You believe that your job, your title, and your position provide you with the primary measure of worth. I understand because that is exactly how I once looked at things.

We all at some point in our lives have had things happen that make us wonder, "Why is this happening to me?" I have come to realize that everything works together. The good, the bad, and the ugly. The good book says that "all things work together for good to those who know and love the Lord." (Romans 8:28). It does not say that all things *are* good – it says, "all things work together *for* good." It also is not for the unbeliever. If you have not come to know the Lord Jesus as your Savior, then the promise in this verse does not apply to you. But it can.

Let's take a moment here today to help you if you are not sure. If you don't have that relationship with the Lord, if you want to know him, you can confess your sins right now. Tell God you are sorry for and turn away from your sins. Believe in your heart that Jesus died for you and rose again. Then you will be saved. (Romans 10:9) Find a good Bible-believing church and study the Word every day. We know all things work for good for us as children of God. So exactly how do they work together? At the time we are enduring our trials, it hardly feels good when we are going through them. But God is working in your life and mine.

Paul was an integral part of the process to help me prepare for my purpose. I did not see it then, but I do now. Paul and I spent five years working together. During those five years, I encountered many difficult times with Paul. He was a Christian too, and he was doing his part to point out where I was not walking upright as a true believer should, even though I did not see it that way at the time.

To prepare means to make ready for use; to get ready, to create in advance.

Our footsteps lead us toward our purpose. We are all here for a purpose and created to do good works. (Ephesians 2:10) When you work hard and do a good job, you want to be acknowledged. That's how I was, and it's how a lot of my previous leaders were. However, with Paul, it was different. He was more focused on the relationships you form just as Dale Carnegie reinforced in his book, *How to Win Friends and Influence People.*

Maybe you are like me and have no trouble getting your job done and doing it successfully, but it does not seem like it's enough to take you to your next level. Such was the case with me. Perhaps this story will help to reveal what could be holding you back from achieving your dreams and finding *your* purpose.

One day, I met with Paul to go over my performance plan. You know, the plan that measures how well you are, or are not, accomplishing your job duties – the goals that the department and company are paying you to achieve. Good news, I was on track. Paul kicked off our meeting by telling me how great I was doing. "You really knocked it out of the park on accomplishing your marketing goals for this quarter, Velma Knowles. I am pleased to see how well things are coming along, but." Isn't there always a "but?" Another shoe to drop? Something to completely reverse all the pride and joy you had going on from having accomplished such a successful goal? He continued, "But, Velma Knowles, you are killing me with all the carnage you are leaving in your wake." You see, I was the proverbial bull in a china shop.

"What are you talking about, Paul? I am working as hard as I can, and it takes a lot of extra work to get everyone inside the department and outside the department to do their part. You really don't understand what I do and how much it takes to get things done around here."

Paul smiled, probably because he knew that I was trying hard to win the support of others only to realize that there was a better way. I would command that others get things done and micro-manage their people to get the expected results. I never really understood what I was doing, although if you knew me then, you would think I did because I had enough confidence to prove it. My blind spots kept me from realizing I should be seeking commitment versus compliance with my team and others.

Paul went on to say how he really knew I could do better. In fact, he was determined to make me better. He wanted me to attend some specific hands-on training. On one side, I did not appreciate his commitment to my personal development (after all, I was well-educated and highly trained), and then on the other side, I thought, well, it wouldn't hurt to achieve another certificate from a training workshop. So, before I knew it, I was enrolled in a 12-week, three hours per week training course. If that alone didn't create an inconvenience, the course was also in the evening, after hours, and on my own time. When you want to grow and become better, you need to be willing to sacrifice something you have for something you don't have so you can achieve what you want.

Chapter 3 – Preparing for Purpose

I really wanted to be a better leader, communicator, and employee, but I just did not know how to go about that. And my pride certainly didn't want to admit that Paul knew the best way to help me achieve my ultimate goal. As I reflect now on my journey, I did not really have anyone other than Paul who was interested enough in helping me to be better at that time.

My journey over the next 12 weeks came with many surprises. For one, every week when I came to the office after my class the previous evening, my team would remark about how well my training was working. They noticed I was acting differently, at least for the first few days after each week's training. Part of our training was to apply on the job what we were learning and then report back the next week. Being the competitive student I was, I began applying everything I was learning so that I could deliver a good report and achieve full points. The interesting thing was my team was noticing a difference, a positive change in my behavior. The best news for me was that Paul, too, was noticing. Little did I know that when you change your attitude and actions, you change your results. Have you ever seen that work for you?

In a meeting, I remember my team member, Suzie, sharing an idea for a new marketing campaign. "We could offer our customers a buy-one and get-one at half price for a limited time, and it will be sure to give us the sales dollars we need to finish this month strong and on budget." My first reaction was to interject and say how that would negatively impact our bottom-line and our potential for bonuses, but this time, I did not say what I was thinking. Instead, I quietly listened and watched how others were just waiting for me to pounce, to revert to the old Velma.

To everyone's amazement, I said: "Suzie, you have a good idea there. Thank you for your willingness to share and think outside the box." Suzie just looked at me, wide-eyed and stunned. I believe she was in total shock. Then, another member on the team, Jan, chimed in and said: "It would really be good to take your offer, Suzie, and target a group of inactive customers, a segment that has not purchased from us in the last 60 days. This would allow us to reach and re-engage our customers who have been dormant for a time." Now I liked the idea even more. The team was alive. We were collaborating. Suzie's idea was great, and so was Jan's. We were not getting any dollars from these disengaged customers, so to get them at even a discount off the product price would be wonderful because we would not be cannibalizing on any existing sales and profit, which would have happened from our active and engaged customers.

I saw the moment as another opportunity to "win friends and influence people," so I jumped in with a smile and gave Jan a high five. We were on a roll now to close the gap in reaching our budget goal. And the best part was we were all enjoying our time working on the project, getting along, there was no damage or wounded egos or hurt feelings; there was only commitment and no need for compliance. I was loving the experience of seeing our team working so well together.

My training was paying off in the form of a more engaged and productive team. I truly owed a lot of my success to Paul for his belief and investment in my growth.

But (and there is always that "but") despite all this success, things did not materialize in a promotion for me. I wanted so much to get that promotion; you know the one you work so hard for only to find that it is awarded to someone else. What was the lesson here? When we are passed over for promotions and opportunities, we sometimes think it's a personal thing. It's not! Really, it's not. As believers, we know that God is in control and nothing happens that is not within His permissive or ordained will. So, either God was allowing me to be passed over for the promotion, or He was orchestrating the events to take place that resulted in me being passed over.

My new training skills were being tested for sure. How do I respond to this embarrassment of not getting the promotion? Everyone was expecting me to be promoted, and so was I. My friends, my family, and everyone in the company. This was horrible, and all the training in the world apparently had done nothing to prepare me for this rejection.

The day came for the big news. An all-hands meeting was called to announce the new promotions. I learned a very valuable lesson that day. Paul was right; the world did not revolve around me. In fact, I learned a greater lesson later in my career, and that is, you don't want to have or do anything that God does not want for you. His ways are always greater than your ways, and His thoughts are higher than your thoughts. While the evidence appeared that I was learning how to be a better leader on the job, in my life God was teaching me to be a better person. He was working on me and my pride, my selfishness, and my competitiveness. I am thankful now for the lessons because as I look back, I can see where His hand was leading me all along. And, with my newfound understanding, I am thankful for those lessons, both inside the office and out!

As my career continued, the company went through a major downsizing. Many loyal and tenured employees lost their jobs. It was a Wednesday morning, I remember it clearly, and I knew that the company was making major decisions. Rumors were flying; everyone was walking on eggshells, sitting on pins and needles, wondering if their names were going to be called to the Human Resources Office for their pink slip. The interesting thing was I did not feel anxious at all. Quite the contrary, I *knew* my name would be called. I fully expected it. You might be wondering what would make me feel that way, considering I had made major improvements in my leadership, built stronger relationships, rebuilt bridges that I had burned, won friends, influenced people and accomplished goals. It turns out when you conquer a mountain with God, He usually puts you in a valley so you can begin your climb to your next mountaintop.

My next climb was about to begin.

About 2:30 on that Wednesday afternoon, I was summoned to the main campus building next door to meet with my manager, Paul. The Human Resources Department, as well as the executive offices and board rooms were located there. I reached for my portfolio and calmly made my way across the parking lot and up a stairway to the Florida conference room. All of the conference rooms had descriptive names rather than simple characters like Conference Room A or B or I or 2.

On my walk to the Florida Room, I reflected on how I was going to handle the news. I knew it was coming for some time because the company had gone through a merger; there were duplicate roles, which meant too many talented people for the work required. It was simple math. If you don't believe that relationships matter, think again, they matter more than anything, and when it comes to performance, a willing attitude beats pure skill every time.

Things had improved for me. But when God has a bigger purpose for you, it does not matter what others might want or what you do. He is going to move heaven and earth to get you where He wants you to be, and such was the case for me. The change that was about to happen had nothing to do with my position or me staying with the company, or if I was doing a good job or not, it was that there was a bigger, more important job for me to do. I just did not know it at the time.

As I entered the Florida Room, I smiled because my eyes locked with Paul's and he did not have his usual Zig Ziglar enthusiastic look on his face. In fact, it was apparent he did not want to do what he was about to do. A part of me wanted to make it easier for him, so I took the attitude of gratitude and gave a nice big hello, smiling as bright as the morning sun. It was not fake, it was real, and it was meant to help Paul through what was going to be a difficult moment for him, probably more difficult for him than for me, now that I think about it. I suppose you could say I am really for those who need help. I knew my manager needed help with this meeting, and even though I was the one being impacted by it, I was also going to be one to help make it as comfortable as I could. No screaming, raising my voice, yelling, or railing against the heartless machine. Rather than say, "Why is this happening to me?" I chose to think, "Why not me?"

I thank the good Lord for the peace that He gave me that day!

Don't get me wrong; I did not want to lose my job, nor could I really afford that loss. I was working hard and needed my salary because, in addition to my own expenses, I was supporting my family in the Bahamas to help them manage their medical bills. Having a job was more important than ever for me.

Paul returned my smile with one of his own and extended his hand to greet me. He then introduced me to the other gray-headed gentleman in the room, "Velma, this is Bob Williams, and he is the Vice President of Human Resources. Please have a seat." I knew it was going to be a different kind of meeting because Paul never called me by my first name only. He would always call me Velma Knowles in his deep bass voice.

As I sat down across from Paul and Bob, the only sound was the roar of the air-conditioning unit pumping out cold air. I calmly looked across the table at these two troubled, nervous gentlemen. It was the first time in a long while that I saw two big guys appear to be so nervous, especially since I am such a small, petite woman. I am hardly an intimidating physical presence; there is certainly nothing to fear from my appearance.

Paul spoke up. 'Velma, you were asked to meet with us because we have, um, some news. We need to let you know that we must let you go. Your last day with the organization will be July 5th. We have a package here with all the details of your severance. We are sorry that we have to separate, but due to a number of synergies, we have to make cuts across the organization."

I quietly listened, making eye contact with both individuals the whole time.

Then Bob spoke.

"We know this is a lot to absorb and have arranged a contact in the Georgia Conference Room if you would like to meet after our meeting. The person there will be able to answer any questions you have on how the executive outplacement services work and help get you started with your next job search. Additionally, we want you to take the rest of this week off because we understand that you will need some time to gather your thoughts." Then Paul asked, "Do you have any questions, Velma?" Again, I could not get over him calling me by just my first name. It felt weird! I answered, "Thank you both for all the work you did to prepare my severance package. I don't have any questions at this time but will reach out over the next two weeks. I know this has been difficult and conversations like this are never easy, so thank you for being so kind to me." I gave them my new training smile and picked up my separation package.

I knew the meeting was over. I stood up, and it was at that point when I extended my hand to Bob. As we shook, Bob said, "Velma, I wish we would have met under different circumstances, because I would really like to get to know you better. You appear to be a great leader."

"Thank you, Bob, it was a pleasure to meet you too," I told him. Then Paul extended his hand and we shook, smiling at each other, probably both remembering all the challenging times, conversations, and periods of heated discussions where we knew our relationship was under way too much stress. Where we knew that there were far too many moments when we were both acting like sandpaper and wood, just not meshing right. But oh, how we had grown in our relationship and become respectful leaders, and yes, even friends.

I made the slow walk back to my building and up to my office. I quietly gathered my things. I had been taking home a number of my personal items over the previous months, so there was not a lot of personal items left to gather. I wrote an 'out of office' message on my email and told my executive assistant I was leaving for the remainder of the day and would be back to the office on Monday. She could reach me on my cell if anything came up.

I took my briefcase and purse and headed down the stairs to my car. Once in my car, driving home, the tears began to fall. The pain of losing my job, and more than that, losing over a decade of purpose, hit me smack in the face. It was the first time that I felt I did not know what I was going to do. What was once my goal to become a vice president, was now only a dream. How could I start over, or worse, try to get such a lofty position when I never had the job before?

Then the tears flowed even more.

My nose got stuffy. I could not breathe clearly, and even worse, I could not see clearly. I eventually pulled over into a busy parking lot and bawled. How could I help my family back in the Bahamas? I suddenly did not have a job, and we needed the money to pay for my aunt's cancer treatment. How could I help when I did not have a job making any money? It was now about someone else. The loss of my job was no longer about me and what I did not have, but more about someone else, my family, and what they needed.

In life when your focus is all about you, I believe you are aiming for success. But when your focus is all about others, you are aiming for significance. Little did I know at the time that God was going to use me to make a significant impact, one that does not require a title, a position, or any money.

In Jeremiah 29:11, it says, "For I know the plans I have for you, declares the Lord, plans not to harm you, but to prosper you, to give you hope and a future." My plan was to climb the corporate ladder and become an executive. God's plan was for me to impact someone's life, for eternity. That someone was my Aunt Winifred, or Aunt Winnie as we affectionally called her. She was the best aunt anyone could ever ask for. She was a gentle spirit, kind-hearted, always focused on what she could do for others; she achieved her significance in serving others. But Aunt Winnie had one thing missing in her life - she did not know the Lord. And now she was in the battle of her life, fighting stage 3 cervical cancer. I was about to learn the valuable lesson that time is much more precious than any silver, gold, or money. There was about to be a silver lining in the cloud of my being downsized, a blessing wrapped within.

After a few days of going through the process of grieving my job loss and all the various emotions that go along with this kind of valley, my focus moved to go home to help care for my Aunt. The family couldn't afford personal, round-the-clock nursing for her as she went through treatments. She needed care constantly. Most importantly, she needed her family around her to feel and know she had all her loved ones close. Aunt Winnie had impacted my life in such a profound way by always placing others above herself. It was not uncommon for her to go without so others could have something they wanted or needed. Now it was my turn to be there for her. The days were so hard. It was painful to watch someone I loved so much wither, lose her appetite, and grow weaker each day. In my heart, there was a bigger concern, one of eternal consequence. I would pray so hard that she would come to know Jesus as her Savior. Everyone in the family lifted her up daily and pleaded for her salvation.

There were days when she would listen as I would read Psalm 23, or I would play podcasts from Dr. Charles Stanley - the Lord is my Shepherd – and she would quietly listen but did not respond to the call. My heart was so heavy, I so wanted her to come to know the Lord, and we felt her time was short as the treatments were not effective, they were not working.

Have you ever wanted someone you love to come to know our Lord? It's an ache in your heart that nothing seems to be able to ease. You want so much to do something, but all you know to do is to pray, have faith, and believe that His will is that none should perish. I had to believe that, and I remember telling the Lord that I know He did not want my Aunt Winnie to perish. So, I held on to my faith in God, it was all I had, but it was enough.

Then came the day. Aunt Winnie called for me and said, "Can you play the Lord is my Shepherd from that Stanley man?" My heart was racing with anticipation that she wanted to hear the message. She was asking for it. I slowly put on the podcast, and we listened to it one more time together. That day her life was forever changed! She accepted Jesus as her Lord and Savior. I was there for that very precious moment. The moment that I had prayed for had come! My prayer was answered. God not only saved my Aunt Winnie, He allowed me the opportunity to be there and see it with my very own eyes, to be used for the greatest role of my life. I had just experienced a moment that was far more important than any job, title, or anything else the world could offer. Aunt Winnie's destiny was forever changed.

Friends, God hears your prayers. (1 John 5:14) He is your good, good Father.

God used all the tough times with Paul to help me grow, to move me to a place where I could impact the lives of others. As I look back, I realize that the long and winding road has brought me to a place where I see a greater purpose for my life.

And in all this, I have also learned that my God and Father has a wonderful way of turning things around. He even has a sense of humor as he accomplishes His will for your life. Remember that vice president position I was seeking? He gave it to me when I stopped seeking it and put Him first in my life.

What are you seeking?

Our purpose in life is to seek Him first and then all these things will be added. I look at myself now and the very thing that I struggled with - people skills, communication, and leadership - are the very things that I am training and speaking on to help people to grow and develop today. God will take your messes and turn them into your message. He did it for me, and He can do it for you, too.

Now I clearly see all along God was indeed preparing me for my purpose. How about you? Do you see how He is preparing you for your purpose? Are you on that mountaintop getting ready for your next valley or are you in your valley getting ready for your next mountaintop? Regardless of where you are on your journey, you are right where God wants you to be.

So, remember this the next time you are called to a difficult meeting or meeting with someone who feels like sandpaper when you know you are definitely wood. Remember, when things don't go as you plan or things don't feel like they are working out for your good, God has a plan. You are on a journey, and while it will take you across many twists and turns, it is preparing you for your purpose.

I learned along the way that my life was not meant solely to have a career, achieve a lofty title in the business world, or to prosper financially. I learned hard lessons that my true purpose was not to serve myself, but rather to serve God by serving others. It took me a while, but I finally and thankfully found a way to live like I never knew I could live before. I finally found a way to live in the presence of the Lord and that He can open any door. A way of living knowing His Way is always best.

You can live this way, too. Even when you feel circumstances are in your control, take time, stop and see that His invisible hand is at work. He is molding you, shaping you, preparing you for your purpose.

About the Author – Velma Knowles

Velma Knowles, Founder and CEO of Leaders Pathway, is a Certified Marketing Executive, DiSC Human Behavior Consultant, and Performance Coach; specializing in the art of Communication, Leadership Development, Organizational Growth, and Association Marketing.

She received her first degree from Webber International University in Babson Park, Florida. Moving to the west coast of Florida, she earned an MBA from the University of Tampa. Her education also includes advanced executive training from The University of Pennsylvania's Wharton School of Business, Bradley University, Disney Institute, and both the American Management Association and the American Marketing Association.

Velma is a former membership association executive with over two decades of national and international experience, including Vice President of Member Experience with the American Automobile Association (AAA). Velma is a Certified Marketing Executive from Sales & Marketing Executives International; a graduate trainer and coach for Dale Carnegie; and a certified speaker, trainer, and coach for the John Maxwell Team.

As a member of Toastmasters International and a Professional Member of the National Speakers Association, Velma is an international keynote speaker who has presented in Australia, Canada, the Bahamas, and across the United States. Her audiences vary from executive boards to elementary students and her expertise includes communication, leadership, team performance, marketing, and membership growth.

As a published author, Velma has written articles for The Leading Edge, The John Maxwell Team Leadership Blog, Winging It, the Official newsletter of the American Birding Association, AAA Going Places and Highroads magazines. Her debut book, *The Valuable Leader: Seven Steps to Greater Growth, Value, and Influence* is an interactive training tool uncovering "the Valuable Leader we all have inside."

An avid birdwatcher, Velma brings that same passion for the birds to the stage as she guides organizations to grow valuable leaders and achieve invaluable results. Her speaking and training techniques leverage insightful and unique storytelling.

Contact Information:

Velma Knowles, MBA, CME
Author, Speaker, Trainer and Coach

President, Leaders Pathway

www.LeadersPathway.com

Chapter 3 – Preparing for Purpose

Chapter 4

Alignments Make the Journey
By Gary Gregory

For as much as we think we know who and what are important in our life at any given moment, each moment gives us new insight into the next. If we pay attention to these moments that pass, we learn and grow through what we go through. It's the journey through our moments and the people God places in our path along the way that makes us truly appreciate what is important.

I realized late in life that God has a plan for my life. He placed people in my life at the right place, at the right moment, and at the right time in each of my journeys. As iron sharpens iron, so a friend sharpens a friend (Proverbs 27:17). This became evident as I made my way through my journeys. I may not have recognized it at the time or in the moment, but it was all part of God's plan. I had no idea that a decision to start a specific journey would turn into valuable relationships over the years. Honestly, I was simply thinking of that moment, that day, that first step out the door. The first step into the next moment started a journey in which I would challenge myself more than I ever thought possible. Challenges that would push me to the limits of what I thought, at the time, were beyond what I was able to physically, emotionally, and spiritually face. That journey would introduce me to a new world I never dreamed and new people that would help me along my journey. There were many times along this journey I wanted to quit, times I wondered why I had decided to do what I was doing and moments that put everything into perspective. My story is one from taking the first step out of the front door to completing an Ironman race. But the most important part of this story is not the finish line of each race, but the journey to the finish line and the people that made the experiences. Finish lines are just that; it's the end of a journey. I may have several medals hanging in my closet from my accomplishments, but the journey turned out to be more than just the medals. It was the people that I encountered that helped me, and the experiences that mattered most in this journey.

A Decision to Start a Journey

One day, it struck me: I realized I was overweight, and my health was spiraling out of control. It clicked with me that if I did not do something about it, and quickly, this slippery slope of obesity would become worse with each passing day. My poor eating habits and work stress did not contribute to a healthy lifestyle. It stemmed from a habit of drinking multiple sodas all day, along with frequent trips to fast food restaurants and long work hours six to seven days a week. Sitting behind a desk for hours on end, stressing over work day in and day out became my routine, my focus, and my entire world. It dawned on me one morning that I had to make a change because I was headed down the wrong path.

Chapter 4 – Alignments Make the Journey

I was scheduled to make a trip to another state for a work conference. I had suffered the night before with a severe case of food poisoning. Because my entire focus was on work, I was determined to make the conference regardless of being up the entire night before extremely sick. I made it to my office early in the morning to finish up a few tasks and collect some items needed for the conference. Still feeling sick, and by this point, weak and woozy, I made it to the bathroom. I recognized I was about to pass out, so I called the police to come get me from the bathroom floor as I was passing out. The next thing I remember was waking up in the hospital with an IV in my arm. My wife was by my side worried sick, relieved that I was fine, and angry with me at the same time as I had chosen work over my health. Within a few days of rest, hydration, and healthy food, I began to feel better. It took about two weeks for me to fully recover from food poisoning and exhaustion. In that time, I had made the decision to work on changing my journey.

My initial decision was to give up soda altogether. It seemed to be a quick-win for better health. I had not been able to drink soda the entire time I was recovering, so this made sense to stop altogether. Within a month, I found myself losing weight. The sodas I was drinking before to keep me awake and give me energy were creating bigger problems; they were adding to my addiction to poor health. As I had conquered one addiction, I felt like this new journey just might have some legs. I felt confident that I could continue to make changes and start a new journey. In a moment I felt invulnerable, that I could do anything, and with a new-found confidence, a new journey was truly about to start.

My First Step Out the Door

With an optimistic outlook on a hot, humid summer day in Corpus Christi, I walked out the front door of my house to continue my journey of getting healthier. Before I left the house, I informed my wife that I was heading outside to go jog. My wife smiled, tried to muffle a giggle, and told me to be safe as I moved towards the front door. She knew that any physical activity for me would be tough but still supported me in my efforts. I returned home ten minutes later, barely able to breathe, let alone stand upright. I was exhausted, sweaty, and worn out. Ten minutes in the hot, humid, Corpus Christi sun took everything out of me. Kindly, my wife brought me a glass of water and told me to go shower and take a nap. I did as she said.

When I woke from my nap, I exclaimed that I loved running and was ready to try it again tomorrow. I was hooked. Running and getting healthier became my focus. This was the decision I was ready to cultivate. It was a journey that I would start alone. It would be much later that I realized that having others by your side would help you become much more successful.

For me, running my 10 minutes here and there became my outlet. When I was not working long hours, I was out running. My entire focus outside of work was running. I knew little about it, except I had to put one foot in front of the other repeatedly. But I knew after enough miles of running, I would be able to continue to lose weight and become a healthier person, for my family and me. But it started as a journey simply about me.

Chapter 4 – Alignments Make the Journey

Within a few years, we decided to make a change and take a leap of faith to move to Dallas. The move was an opportunity to grow my career and improve our family life. Little did I know it would be in Dallas that my journey of better health would become even more significant. And it would be here that I would meet the people that God had placed in my life at the right time and place to help me in my journey.

When I first arrived in Dallas, I discovered the 5k race. The 5k race is 3.2 miles. For me, this was a new challenge. At the moment in my health and fitness journey, it appeared to me that this was the pinnacle of what I could accomplish. The 5k was a race that stretched farther than I had ever run before. After participating in a few 5k races, I become complacent and shared with myself that I would be happy training and competing in the 5k race format. I mean, it was exciting, it was far, and I could do it alone. And that was good enough for me.

A Needed Push

It was within a few months that, through my wife, I met a personal trainer who had an extra bicycle and some free time to share. This accidental connection set forth another new journey. As I was content with running the 5k races, my new personal trainer friend had other plans. Brian decided that if I could do a 5k race, then I could add a few other things into the mix. With his borrowed bike, I started cycling as well. He allowed me to take his bike home and start practicing.

On several occasions, I rode the bike around the neighborhood. In my perspective, my bike rides were extremely long. Brian would hold back his amusement when

I shared with him proudly that I had ridden up to 3 miles on the bike. Feeling sorry for me, Brian continued to push me to extend the mileage. It took several visits to a local riding area for me to finally get comfortable riding a bike and longer distances. It wasn't long that the 3 miles on the bike turned into 5 miles, then into 10 miles, then onto 15 miles. With each new mile on the bike, I felt I had pushed my limits and conquered new distances.

Once I conquered the extra mileage on the bike, and I could run a 5k, Brian persuaded me to combine a long bike ride and a run together. I asked if he meant bike on a Saturday and then run on a Sunday. Brian chuckled and shared that it would be on the same day, and in fact, right after we finished riding, we would start running. At that point, I started questioning our friendship because he was certainly suggesting something that could not be done because I knew how I felt after riding a few miles on the bike. And to suggest running right afterward was crazy. Sure enough, the next weekend Brian took me back to our local riding area, this time with a bike and running shoes. I was questioning my decision to join Brian on this new journey. But there I was because he believed I could do this.

After riding 10 miles, we brought our bike back to the cars, locked them up, and put on our running shoes. My heart was racing, and panic started to kick in as I thought what it would be like to start running after such a long bike ride.

With a water bottle in my hand and running shoes on my feet, we took off running. Or at least as close to running as I could muster. My legs felt like mush while running after the bike ride. It was a struggle to make my legs do what I wanted to do. After what felt like hours of running, we made it back to our starting point. Those seemingly hours of running were simply about 15 minutes, about 1 ½ miles. I could not believe that I had done that. I looked at Brian with what I am sure was a pathetic-looking and exhausted face. Between my huffing and puffing, I thanked him for pushing me to do what I thought I could not. I could feel a swell of confidence build up. Confidence that I could push my limits and go beyond what I thought I could not do.

After several months of riding more and more miles and then running more and more after each bike ride, it felt easier and easier. Brian reminded me that it doesn't get easier; you just get stronger. At that moment, Brian uttered the word that would eventually take me to yet another level of challenges: triathlons. I vaguely knew what a triathlon was but had no idea how impactful it would become. Brian suggested that I start swimming along with the riding and running. The suggestion of the three appeared to be undoable. But, since Brian had not steered me wrong so far, off I traversed to the local natatorium to start swimming. I had not swum since I was a kid and knew this type of swimming would be a struggle.

After getting in the pool at 5 am with the swim class, it turned out I knew what I was talking about. Getting in my laps was a struggle as I gasped for breath and felt my lungs burn like never before. But I knew if I could ride a bike for miles and then run for additional mileage, I could conquer the swim.

After months of swimming in the pool, cycling and running, Brian suggested we tie it all together for a local triathlon race. A triathlon is a race in which a group of people swim, bike, and then run in consecutive order to the finish line. There are various distances to triathlons race, but what Brian was suggesting was a sprint. The shortest of the triathlon race series. It was a scary proposition, but at this point, my confidence was riding high. Sure enough, within a few days, I was signed up for my first triathlon race.

Days before the race, I picked up my race packet at a local store. I made it to the store, found the check-in table, and picked up my packet. At that point, the butterflies started. I saw all the other athletes around picking up their packets as well. I felt in my mind that I could not compete with these other amazing athletes around me. Doubt started creeping in.

The morning before the race, I was a complete wreck, nervous as I could be. I must have packed and re-packed all my racing gear a hundred times so as not to forget anything. My stomach was in knots, and I could not sleep at all that night.

Triathlon races typically start early in the morning to allow time for all the athletes to complete the race within a certain time frame. I showed up before sunrise with Brian at the transition area with my bicycle, helmet, and racing gear that had been checked at least a dozen times before I left the house in the morning.

Brian showed me how to set up my transition space with my bike, helmet, and running shoes, among other items.

Chapter 4 – Alignments Make the Journey

We checked and rechecked before heading to the swim start. While walking to the swim start, Brian noticed I was getting extremely nervous. I confided that I was scared and not sure I could do this. I didn't think I belonged in the same group with all these other athletes. Brian stopped me and looked at me. He said to me that you only need to compete against yourself and race as we have trained. That's all. I nodded and thanked him for that.

I was nervous standing in line to jump in the swimming pool to start the race but grew in confidence that I could do this triathlon thing. Eventually, it was my turn to jump in the pool and start my race. I jumped into the cold swimming pool water feet first, emerged with a big gasp, and began to race like I had trained. After several laps up and down and through the pool, being swum over, kicked, and hit by other swimmers, I climbed out of the pool with just a few bruises. I was so dizzy that I nearly fell over running to the transition area to get my bike. Fumbling through getting my proper gear on, I made my way out on the bike. The sun was rising over the horizon, and the cool morning air began to heat up. The water from the pool quickly evaporated and turned to sweat. Making my way through the bike course after being passed by dozens of people, I made it back to the transition area to run.

I witnessed all the other bikes back in the transition area, which meant there were a lot of people already out running. It didn't matter how far back I was; this race was for me. Sitting down next to my bike, I changed my gear to get ready for the run. After a deep breath, I stood up and started running. By this time my lungs were burning, my legs were burning, but my desire to complete this race was burning more. Running and walking got me to the finish line. There was Brian waiting and cheering for me as I passed over the timing mat. I kept walking because I knew if I stopped moving, I would fall over. Brian walked with me and told me that I did it. I did it. It was an incredible moment. This journey had brought me to my first of many finish lines.

Learning the Team Concept

After that first triathlon, I was hooked. I could not wait to race another triathlon. And I did, many more times. Each race I started to get better, faster, and stronger. This journey was growing with each race.

During a random conversation with a wonderful lady from work, I mentioned that I was racing in triathlons. Her eyes got really big when I said triathlon. She mentioned that her son, Scott, was managing a triathlon race team in the area. The next day her son called me and set up a meeting to discuss joining his racing team. A simple connection turned into an amazing opportunity. After meeting with Scott, I joined his triathlon racing team and became a sponsored athlete. This experience was incredible because I was able to join a group of athletes, that a few years ago, I thought I did not belong.

It was not long under the supervision and encouragement of Scott that my shorter sprint triathlon races turned into Olympic distance. An Olympic distance is twice the distance of a sprint. Within the team, we were able to pull from each other's strengths to make each other better along the way. During a race, it was our responsibility to encourage one another, as well as push and pull each other along the way. This once solo sport became a team sport to get each other to the finish line.

Perfecting the Technical

In the triathlon racing team, I met two incredible athletes that would become more than just team members; they became friends. We trained together, we held each other accountable, and we pushed each other to get better.

Amy was an amazing swimmer. It took one swim lesson from Amy to improve my swimming form and improve my swim time. Archie was incredible on the bike. He helped me perfect my form and improve specific aspects of my cycling. The greatest part about being part of this team was that we cheered each other on during training and the races. We shared knowledge, training plans, encouragement, and laughs along the way. If one was down, we encouraged each other. If another was racing at their peak, we cheered them on. This racing team was a family.

It wasn't long that we eyed the next level of triathlon racing, the Half Ironman. Even though it is a Half, don't let that fool you. A Half Ironman is 70.3 miles of pure racing. We all traveled to Galveston to race in our first Half Ironman after months of intense training. This out of town adventure was beyond anything we had ever done before. It was an ocean swim, a bike on the windy coast, and a run during the heat of a humid day. It did not matter that I was out of my element and that I would more than likely not see my teammates except for a passing moment during the race, we all knew we were being cheered on by each other.

Chapter 4 – Alignments Make the Journey

The morning started with questionable conditions for a race with rough and choppy water in the bay, higher than normal winds, and anticipated hotter than normal temperatures. I was questioning starting the race, knowing it would be more than extremely difficult to finish under optimal weather conditions, but these weather conditions were going to make it even beyond what we had ever attempted before.

Without the encouragement of each other before the race, the comradery from my teammates in this race would not have happened. Under my newfound confidence, I put my toe on the starting line and ended up finishing the race. It was not easy, but this journey happened with the help of my team family.

Racing Smart

Along the way of my racing, I met Brent. Brent was the husband of my wife's coworker. This was another accidental meeting that created a partnership that would continue to push my limits. Brent was an incredible athlete. He was a great swimmer, great at cycling, and great at running. There was nothing that Brent could not do. And most notably, nothing he could not do better and faster than me. That was exactly what I needed for a training partner. Brent and I started training together. We biked and ran together every free moment we could find. Brent was super kind as he would wait for me to catch up with him as we trained. On several occasions, Brent would fall back with me as the remaining group of cyclists rode on, or as runners turned the corner and ran on ahead. I was determined to keep pushing on, even when there were moments I had nothing left in me. Brent had a way to kindly push me beyond my limits during each training ride or run.

We ended up traveling to several locations to race together. Brent always knew how to create a methodical approach to his training and racing. I learned so much from him about how to become a better racer through an analytical and thoughtful approach. Racing became a combination of pure, physical grit combined with thoughtful planning. This approach was new to me. It again transformed my racing and pushed my limits in yet another way. Racing smart became a new strategy with Brent. God placed Brent on my journey to refine my skill as, "If the ax is dull and it's edge unsharpened, more strength is needed, but skill will bring success." (Ecclesiastes 10:10 NIV). We finished a lot of races together, usually with me right behind him. And we continued to get better.

Creating Endurance

As I began to improve my racing with each person and challenge I met, I was fortunate enough to meet another person to influence my racing. Hamlin was another accidental meeting. He happened to be another fellow teacher with my wife. Hamlin is one of those individuals that is superhuman when it comes to running and racing. The most incredible thing about Hamlin is that running comes so natural to him. I followed Hamlin around as best I could to learn how he was able to run and race with the greatest of ease. He would convince me to take on challenges that would normally seem absurd. But as it would happen, there I was tackling and completing his challenges. No matter how hard I pushed myself, I could never beat Hamlin. But that never stopped me from trying. I knew if I was going to get better, then I needed to surround myself with people like Brent and Hamlin that were way better than me. Under his influence, I was able to start running mile after mile. And each mile continued to get faster. With Hamlin and Brent, we traveled to even more races, pushing our limits with each event. Some of the most difficult racing I was challenged with was in Lubbock and in the grasslands outside of Ft. Worth. No matter how challenging the races were ahead of us, it was with Hamlin's and Brent's support that we made the finish line at each race.

Ironman Journey

After several years of pushing my limits with the 5k, 10k, half marathons, marathons, running races, 100-mile bike rides, trail runs, sprints, Olympic and Half Ironman distance triathlons, it was time to focus on the ultimate race. The Ironman race: which is 140.6 miles of racing – 2.4 miles of swimming, 112 miles of cycling and 26.2 miles of running. With a 17-hour cut off time, yes, 17 hours to complete a 140.6-mile race, it was a daunting task at best. But I knew from all my training and time spent with amazing athletes that it seemed like something that was obtainable for someone that was once overweight and barely able to manage 10 minutes of walking/jogging.

The day came to make the decision to sign up for the race, one year in advance. I entered all my registration information in the computer one evening and I was ready to hit the enter button. Before I did, I looked at my wife and asked if she was ready to continue to support me for another year of training for a race that was, for me, the pinnacle of my journey so far. With a smile I had not seen since I took those first steps out the door one hot and humid day in Corpus Christi, she said yes. At that moment, with those butterflies I had not felt since my first race, I pressed the submit registration button for the Ironman Louisville, Kentucky race. And so, it started a year of training to prepare for a race that I had 17 hours to complete. Brent and I began our training for the race. For this journey, my focus was, "Whatever you do, work at it with all your heart, as working for the Lord" (Colossians 3:23).

Day after day we would swim, bike, and run together. I would evaluate my progress and discuss it with Brent along the way. There were several good days and several bad days of training. It took Brent and our fellow training partners to keep me motivated and on course for our goal. Finally, it was time to make our drive from Dallas to Louisville. Just like my first race, I packed and re-packed my gear a dozen times to make sure I had everything I needed, plus a few back-ups. A few days before the race, we loaded up Brent's SUV, and we hit the road. The miles and conversations to Louisville seemed to fly by. We made it to Louisville within two days of driving. Our housing was provided by a friend from work that learned of our adventure. We stayed with her family just outside of town within a short drive of the race start.

A day before the race, it was time to check in. When we arrived at the convention center for the event, there were hundreds and hundreds of athletes from all over the US and world. I could feel the nerves starting to grow. The familiar questions started swirling around my head, did I have enough, was I good enough to be in the same group as these other amazing athletes?

I checked in for the race, received my racing number and all the additional items needed. Brent and I walked to the bike check-in area along with a thousand others. Finding my bike rack spot, I positioned my bike and then dropped off my transition bags in the field of other bags. Brent and I walked around for a while, looked over the starting line, course markings and the Ohio River. I tried to release the nervous energy with small talk and race strategy, but deep down I was still questioning if I was able to make the distance that I had never attempted before. When we finished with all the pre-race setup and location scouting, it was getting close to dinner time. Heading back to our place for the night, we stopped at a Dairy Queen on the way. In a moment of comfort, the large Blizzard with M&Ms brought a sense of relief and laughter as we spotted another Ironman athlete eating the same thing at the next table.

It was nearly impossible to sleep that night. The alarm sounded at 3:30am waking me from my spotty moments of sleep. Dressing in my race gear placed out the night before, I grabbed my gear bag and headed out the door choking down a bagel the best I could.

Arriving at the race site before sunrise, a thousand athletes were all milling about checking on last-minute preparations and making the last adjustments for the day ahead. Nervous conversation filled the air along with the morning dew.

Chapter 4 – Alignments Make the Journey

It was time to make our way to the swim start line. This race had a time trial start, allowing about three people to jump into the river at a time as opposed to the thousand athletes racing to the water's edge all at once. Brent and I stood in line, and we inched closer to the starting dock. We shook hands, hugged it out, and wished each other the best of luck because after jumping in the water, we would more than likely not see each other until the end of the race.

I stepped on the dock primed and filled with nerves to start this race. A year of training was about to be tested. The next step would not be out the door, but into the Ohio River to start a 140.6-mile journey of swimming, biking, and running. The volunteer looked at me, entered my race number into their computer and said, "GO!" It was indeed "GO" time. My determination was found in "Do you know that in a race all runners run, but only one gets the prize? Run in such a way as to get the prize" (1 Corinthians 9:24). The prize was waiting at the end of this journey.

I jumped into the water feet first, emerged with a big gasp of breath, and started swimming. Surrounded by hundreds of swimmers, it was time to start applying all the training and race how I trained. After what seemed like a short eternity, I arrived at the end of the swim section. Next to me at the end of the swim was one of my previous teammates climbing out of the water at the same time. We both looked at each other, smiled, and encouraged each other on as we headed to the bikes. Quickly changing into my cycling gear and running to find my bike among the thousand other bikes added to the excitement of this next transition. I found my bike and ran with it to the bike mounting line. As I reached the mounting line, there in the spectator crowds was the family Brent and I were staying with, cheering me on. That moment of cheering filled my spirit and fueled me on to the next section of the race.

The bike portion of the race ahead was 112 miles of hills and the hot, humid sun. My determination was solid by this point. I settled into the bike, monitored my breathing, hydration, and calorie intake to ensure I could make it through. My focus was broken only by the smattering of crowds gathered cheering on all the cyclist along the course. As I approached 100 miles on the bike, I recognized that I had never ridden farther than 102 miles at one time. Again, the nerves shot through me, but I knew it would just be another barrier to break. As I passed 102 miles into uncharted distances on the bike, I broke yet another barrier ahead of me and the remaining 10 miles would be simple. Riding up to the final transition, a huge sense of relief washed over me. One more portion of the race remained, a full 26.2 mile run.

Placing my bike on the rack and changing into my running gear, I was ready to tackle this last section of the Ironman. My legs did not have the same anticipation of readiness. My movement and stride struggled at best for the first few miles as I worked hard to get my muscles to convert from a cycling motion to a running motion. Different muscles worked hard to engage and move forward. After a few miles on the run, I felt something in my sock that was causing me extreme irritation. I had to stop to fix my sock or I knew I would cause injury to my foot. As I stopped and wobbled to maintain an upright position as best I could, I took my shoe and sock off. Shaking my sock, a spectator from the race ran up and offered me his socks. It was so shocking and touching that a stranger would offer me his pair of socks so that I could finish this race. I was touched. Emotions were already high from the sheer exhaustion, and I choked back a tear. I politely declined the stranger's socks, fixed my own sock, and slipped on my shoe again. With a high five from the stranger, I continued my run.

Along the marathon are aid stations set up with volunteers with encouragement, drinks, and food. Each aid station presented an oasis of friendly encouraging faces that offered any and all sustenance needed. At this point in the race, I needed energy. Water, Cokes, cups of chicken broth, and cookies were my preferred choice of food along with a random high five.

The miles passed with a combination of running and jogging along the route. Each runner, volunteer, and spectator cheered me on and filled my spirit with that much more determination. Running through the two 13-mile loops of the course I knew at this point, this journey was coming to an end. My watch showed how close I was getting with each step, each minute that passed. I could finally see the final turn to head to the finish line. Running down the finish chute hit me hard. It wasn't the exhaustion at this point that made it hard to breathe, it was sheer emotion of the culmination of a year of training for this moment and the years and friends that helped me get to this point. Hundreds of people crowded the finish line chute. The deafening cheers and extended hands for high fives was overwhelming. It was hard to choke back the tears. The finish line carpet and cheering people were surreal, and I felt like I was floating for the last 100 yards.

I realized, after crossing the finish line in downtown Louisville, KY, after 140.6 miles of sheer determination, after hearing my name called as an Ironman and receiving the Ironman medal, all I wanted was to find Brent. I wanted to share the accomplishment with my friend, to share the results of the journey with him that made all this possible.

Weaving through the crowds of volunteers and fellow Ironman finishers, I finally found Brent. Finding each other, we both stopped, exhaled a breath of relief and gave each other a big hug. In that moment I had an epiphany. The finish line was the ultimate end for this journey, and I was ecstatic to get to the finish line, but the journey with Brent and with all the people that God had placed in my life, was the most important.

Now that this specific journey had concluded, I needed to find a new journey, new people to connect with and grow. But this time, I faced a fork in the road of my journey. I had so many people help me along the way to get to the finish line of my journey, it was time for me to return the favor. I would find myself taking a step out my front door on a new journey to help others reach their finish line.

For me, it is incredible how a simple decision to walk out the door on a hot and humid day in Corpus Christi led me on a journey that would change my life and give me the opportunity to meet so many wonderful people along the way. After all, it was not all about me on this journey.

The common denominator on my journey was the people I met along the way that helped me get better. This journey would not have been possible without this group of people God had put in my life. My wife supported me as I chased my crazy journeys beyond the first step out the door and the athletes made me better. I needed each person along the way at the time and the place I met them for a specific purpose. Even in an individual sport as triathlons, it takes a group of the right connections to help get you to the finish line.

I know through my experiences that whatever decision I make and journey I may take, I will find the right connections at the right place and at the right time to make the best things happen. And those people I surround myself with will always be stronger, faster, smarter, and better than me in some capacity. But at the same time, it is my responsibility to help others on their journeys as well, "so I run with purpose in every step" (1 Corinthians 9:26 NIV). No matter the journey, if you want it to be successful, it is a team sport with God and the people He places in your path. "He gives power to the weak and strength to the powerless. Even the youths will become weak and tired, young men will fall in exhaustion. But those who trust in the Lord will find new strength." (Isaiah 40:29-31)

Our journeys will give us insight as to what is most important at any given moment. Paying attention on your journey will give you great perspective, new connections, and stronger appreciation for what is most important. It's the alignments that God places in your path on the journey, not the destination that makes each journey special and meaningful.

About the Author – Gary Gregory

I am first and foremost a servant of Jesus Christ our Savior. For over 25 years I have shared my life with my incredible wife who has put up with all my crazy dreams and terrible dancing. God has blessed us with four incredible children along with every other neighborhood kid that runs in and out of our front door and back door.

Growing up in Houston in a quiet suburban neighborhood with two solid and supportive parents likened to June and Ward Cleaver, I was a quiet nerdy kid throughout school afraid to go beyond my boundaries and make mistakes. I eventually ventured to the University of Houston where a new world was presented beyond the suburbs and I decided to change when I got to college (though I never quite lost the nerdy description if you ask many of my friends).

While in college I attempted to experience most everything available except studying. So distracted by all the new experiences and opportunities, my school took second seat. Changing majors from graphic communications to business was when I started to find my stride and eventually my future wife (and a college degree).

After graduating college and getting married, I jumped in work. I worked retail and traveled the country teaching computer software from Houston, moved to El Paso and taught GED English and worked a BINGO hall, moved to Corpus Christi to manage student housing and valet park cars and finally to Dallas to manage multi-family housing. Eventually, I started my amateur racing experiences and personal training business out of Dallas. Each jump was an attempt to fill a need that I could not fill.

It was not until my wife dragged me to church kicking and screaming in 2016 that I began to find out what was most important in my life. My eyes were open, and I realized what I was missing, the need I was trying to fill. Through Pastor Keith Craft and the connections made through Elevate Life Church, I devoted my life to better things. Each day is a chance to fight the good fight alongside God, my wife, my children and my family of choice. My boundaries and opportunities now are limitless.

For more motivation, inspiration or information visit: www.thegarygregory.com

Chapter 4 – Alignments Make the Journey

Chapter 5

Believe in the *You* God Created
By Glenn Keller

In my first book, *Moving My Mountains: A Journey to Peace from Codependency*, I wrote about dealing with the symptoms of codependency. However, that wasn't my first thought. I started to write about being a full-blown codependent. It wasn't until a dear friend helped me realize we are not born with that stuff; certain issues and habits that we have are picked up in life. We weren't born with a little pouch that contained codependency no more than we were born with low self-esteem or issues. Yet, I was ready to take ownership of something God did not give me at birth. I had claimed a fact that wasn't even a fact, and it was that I, Glenn Calvin Keller, was codependent. This just seems like a good place to say that "the devil is a lie!" So many of the issues that we face and the things that try to overcome us are not issues that God created or placed in us. So much of the baggage that we carry we didn't come into the world with, we actually picked it up along the way.

The *you* that God created was made in the likeness and image of God. Please forgive me if I can't go into detail describing God's likeness or image because I imagine God's likeness and image to be more than my mind can even comprehend. Yet that is the likeness that you and I came into this world with. It was the image you and I had the day that we were born. If we had parents that brought us to church as kids, we learned at a young age that we were all special in God's sight. It's a good thing that I'm writing and not singing, but I'm reminded of the words to a song that said, "Jesus loves the little children. All the children of the world. Red, yellow, black, and white, they are precious in His sight. Jesus loves the little children of the world."

Allow me to talk a little to the men about believing in the *you* God created. Brothers, this is going to call for a little imagination on our part. Okay, imagine with me if you will, a God that was so awesome that He actually spoke this entire world and everything in it into existence. Which, to me, says God did it all by Himself. This is where I see man as being so important that He didn't want to just speak man into existence, nor did God want to go at it alone. I came to the conclusion that God did not want to create man alone for God said, and I quote, "let us make man." (Genesis 1:26) A little later on the Bible says the Lord God formed man out of the dust of the ground, and breathed into his nostrils the breath of life, and man became a living soul. (Genesis 2:7) This is where my imagination kicks into overdrive, and maybe you won't get as excited as I did when I read this in God's Word. The God of the universe. The God of Abraham, Isaac, and Jacob got down on His hands and knees as if He were in a sandbox and began to form man out of the dust of the earth. God began pulling dirt towards Him like a master sculpture and started to form the different parts of a man's body. I can imagine God forming the head, the eyes, the nose, the mouth, the neck, the shoulders, the arms, the hands, the fingers, the torso, the thighs, the knees, the ankles, the feet, and then the toes. Okay, I think you get the picture. I believe that I have a very vivid imagination, but I can't even begin to imagine how the heart, the liver, the kidneys, the lungs, and the stomach were put into place. As if all of this wasn't amazing enough, God performed the first mouth-to-mouth. My imagination is being overwhelmed again because God then leaned over and breathed into man's nostrils the breath of life, and man became a living soul. How awesome is that? How special is that? That is the *you* God created.

My sisters, I did not forget about you. If God were going to create a companion or helpmate for man, some might think God would have consulted man and about what would please him. Then how would man have described something he had never seen before? Since God really didn't need the man's opinion or help, God just put man to sleep, performed the first surgery by removing a rib from the man's side, and created the woman. In all of God's creation and until the present day, there has not been a creation more beautiful than the woman. I remain impressed by the fact that God didn't even bring the woman into the picture until everything was finished. By the way, when God called you the weaker vessel, it wasn't to say that you are a lesser vessel. It's just to say you are fragile and should be covered and protected.

Well, what am I saying? I'm searching for the words that will help explain how awesome the *you* that God created really is. I've spent what seems like my entire life in church. There is a phrase that I've heard people use for what seems like my entire life. The phrase is "I'm waiting on The Lord."

This phrase has been used in every conceivable way. At times, this phrase may make it seem like God is the butler or the bellhop. If not careful, it can make God seem like an enabler. It's as if we are expecting God to show up at the door of our hotel room like room service with the things that we want and desire in life. Even worse, the truly impatient think that God is going to show up like a famous pizza chain that promised delivery in 30 minutes or less. Don't get me wrong, I get what people are saying when they say they are "waiting on The Lord." There is an expectation that The Lord will lead and guide us. The Bible tells us that God will direct our path. (Proverbs 16:9) For those who may feel like you've been waiting on The Lord forever and haven't gotten a response, have you ever taken a moment to consider that The Lord may just be waiting on you?

When it seems like God has not heard us or that He's not even listening, or worse, that He doesn't even care, stop for a moment and think of the possibility that God has been waiting on you. You may ask, "Why would The Lord be waiting on me?" It's very possible that The Lord has been waiting on you and me to use the many gifts and talents that He has bestowed upon us and placed inside of us in order that we might have the things that we ask Him for. I don't believe for a minute that The Lord promised us He would supply all of our needs and even that He would be our provider in order to enable us to be idle. I believe miracles are the things only God performs and the other things we obtain in life are up to us. The Lord didn't put this massive computer with an unlimited hard drive between our ears so that He could turn around and figure out everything for us.

The God that created you also trusts His creation. It may be similar to the way a mother trusts her baby taking his or her first steps. At that point in our lives, we have no idea whether we can take those first steps. We don't even know what steps are at that point. However, mom not only knew what steps were, but she also knows that we can do it. All of us struggled in those early years to walk because we never took our hands off of the coffee table or that sofa. When we did get to the end of the coffee table, it was time to drop down and start crawling again because, at that stage of the process, we had absolutely no confidence that we could perform the task we now take for granted without assistance.

The doctors that have come up with cures for countless diseases have done so using all of their God-given gifts, talents, and facilities. When we were discharged from the hospital, we were not stamped or labeled doctor, lawyer, professor, teacher, engineer, scientist, or author, to name a few. All of that was yet to be determined. I wonder if it's safe to say that none of us started out with a real advantage other than the fact that the same God created us all. There may have been some perceived advantages depending on what side of town you grew up on or what side of the tracks you were born on, yet on that day that we took that first breath outside of our mother's womb, it was as level of a playing field as there would ever be in our lives. I tread lightly here because some would think, for instance, that the child born with two arms, two legs, ten fingers, and ten toes would have an advantage. I'll refer to that as a perceived advantage. I've seen and read about what those who have been born without any legs or arms have been able to accomplish in their lives which have left me speechless, with my mouth hanging open, and in tears, I might add.

The *you* God created has an unlimited capacity to learn, along with unlimited potential, abilities, and capabilities. One of my favorite passages of Scripture from the Bible says, "to Him that is able to do exceedingly and abundantly above all that we can ask or think according to the power that works in us." (Ephesians 3:20) I really love the portion of that Scripture that says, "according to the power that works in us." So if I got this right, and I'm by no stretch of the imagination a theologian, God is able to do what He does, which is above all you and I can ask and think, based on a power that's already in you and me. I'm excited that there is a power working in you and me that, once activated, opens the door for God to bless us in ways we can't even begin to imagine. Trusting in the *you* God created will blow your mind. If we are not doing great things in our life, it's because we don't think we can or simply don't believe that we can.

We can if we believe that we can. In Mark 9:23-24 Jesus said unto him, "If you can believe, all things are possible to him who believes." Immediately the father of the child cried out and said with tears, "Lord, I believe, help my unbelief!" Just like this man that the Bible speaks about, we can ask God to help our unbelief, the unbelief that inhibits you from believing the *you* that God created. Our faith in God and what He can do is intact. We have no problem having the faith to believe that God can do anything but fail. Where is your faith in the *you* God created?

Paul helps us get rid of that notion that God does it all for us. Paul actually said, "I (Paul) can do all things through Christ which strengthens me." (Philippians 4:13) In other words, Paul can, you can, and I can do all things through Christ who strengthens us. Not that Christ does it for you, but that you can do it through the Christ that wakes you up each day. The Christ that gives you the mobility of your limbs. There were some lyrics in an old secular song that said, "show me what you're working with." I may be a little facetious, but does the God who created you look down from Heaven every day and say, "Show Me what you're working with?" After all, it's not like God doesn't already know what you're working with. "Show Me what you're doing with the many tools that I've given you." What do we do with the gifts and talents that God has placed inside of each and every one of us? Make no mistake about it, we all have something. God created us with something that, when activated and used to the fullest, would not only change our lives, but the lives of others, and could even change the world.

I would like to take a break right here for a testimony. I never once thought about being an author when I was growing up. However, this is my third book project inside of 4 years, and the first book was a #1 bestseller. I'm also a successful business owner and a Zig Ziglar certified speaker and trainer, none of which I considered doing with only a high school diploma. I want you to believe in the *you* that God has created because amazing things have happened in my life since I began to believe in the me that God created. There is a parable in the Bible that seems to show somewhat of a disdain for those unwilling to use the talents that they have been given. (Matthew 25:14-30) The parable says three people were given money. The two people that used their talents were essentially able to double the money given to them. The one that didn't use his talent had the money taken away from him. One of my greatest fears in life has been that if I didn't use my gifts that I would ultimately end up losing them.

Through the wonders of mass media, we learn about so many incredibly talented people. We read about these people in books, on the internet and even watch them on television. People that have done great, amazing, and astonishing things. They are people God created just like He created you and me. People that are tall, short, fat, skinny, rich, poor; whose skin is red, yellow, black, white, and brown.

Just as God created these amazing people, he created you. I'm convinced that you will never go wrong believing in the *you* that God created. I believe that when God brought you into this world that He placed a bet on you. God had so much confidence in you that His bet in Deuteronomy 28:12-13 was that you would be the head and not the tail, above and not beneath, the lender and not the borrower. God was so sure of His creation He bet you would be an overcomer. An overcomer of everything that would try to come against you.

God shielding you would have been like Him putting His thumb on the scale. God had to allow you to operate under something called free will. Had God done everything for you, it would be like exercising under the influence. In order for God to be betting on you, there had to be someone betting against you. God knew that you were fearfully and wonderfully made. The enemy was betting that you weren't. God has always been willing to bet on the *you* that He created. Maybe in this case, God's bet is being considered an outside bet. God needed you to believe in and bet on the *you* He created.

God even accounted for the pain you would encounter. At the point you felt like the pain was unbearable and you would throw in the towel, the God who created you would whisper in your ear "My grace is sufficient."

Before you think that I have lost my whole mind talking about The God who created you placing a bet on you, believe me, I haven't. Let me remind you of our brother Job. That's right, Job. Please allow me to paraphrase. Satan assumed that Job was only serving God because of how God had blessed him. Satan was so convinced that he wanted to bet God that if God were to allow him to take away those blessings, that Job would curse God. Well, God being confident in the Job He created took that bet. God was so confident in the Job that He created that he didn't even tell Job about the bet. God didn't feel the need to give Job a pep talk. God didn't feel the need to tell Job, "Look, I'm betting on you, Job, and I don't need to tell you how this is going to look if I lose."

Had satan known God like Job knew God, satan would have known that was a sucker bet. God allowed, and I said allowed because satan didn't have the power he thought he had, and surely not the power we seem to think he has sometimes. I say that because if satan had any power, he would not have needed prior approval or permission to afflict Job. Yet satan was allowed to rob Job of most, if not all, of his worldly possessions, including his children. Even after Job lost everything, he still didn't curse the God that created him. As a matter of fact, I believe Job kind of added insult to injury. Not only did Job not curse God, but in spite of what had happened, Job blessed God. The Job that God created said, "The Lord gives and the Lord takes away, blessed be the name of The Lord" (Job 1:21). Well, why satan wouldn't quit while he was behind is beyond my understanding. Okay, this no power, no authority satan went back to God, seeking permission this time to afflict Job's body. Even after afflicting Job's body, Job would not curse God. Job stood up and said, "though He slay me yet will I trust Him." (Job 13:15) Not only did Job believe in the Job God had created, but God also demonstrated a whole-hearted belief in the Job He had created.

You have an enemy that is counting on you not believing in the *you* that God created. Not believing in the *you* that God created you hinders you from getting to your destiny. It's the thing that could be stopping you from being, doing, and having everything that God intended for you to have in this life. God has placed everything in this world that we will ever need. There is nothing new being created. Scientists are taking things that are already here and putting them together with other things that are already here to form new things, but nothing new is being created.

What you need to be successful is already here, you just have to find it. Not everybody is going to be a scientist. Somebody makes a better sweet potato pie than anybody else in the world. Somewhere in between scientist and baker lies God's plan and purpose for your life. It takes getting up every day, having faith in God, and believing in the *you* that

God created. Make no mistake, there are going to be obstacles. I once heard my mentor Zig Ziglar say, "By the time a child reaches 18 years old they've been told 148,000 times what they can't do." That can be overcome when they are convinced to believe in the *them* that God created. Then they can begin to believe like Paul that I can do all things through Christ who strengthens me.

You've got to believe in yourself when no one else will. Les Brown tells a story of a little boy in the third grade sitting at his desk working. The teacher passes by his desk and asks what he is working on. The little boy replies, "I'm painting a picture of God." The teacher then replies, "Nobody knows what God looks like." The young boy then says, "They will in a minute!" You've got to believe in yourself when no one else will.

Believing in the *you* God created can get you everything you desire in this life. Believing in the God that created you and His Son Jesus will get you everything in the next life.

About the Author – Glenn C. Keller Sr.

My name is Glenn C. Keller, Sr. and I was born in New Orleans, LA; home of The New Orleans Saints, Mardi Gras and affectionately known as, The Big Easy. I have one sister; Carol Ann Keller, two sons; TaDaro L. Keller and Glenn C. Keller, Jr.

I grew up in church, which was not an option back then, and I am grateful. I was educated in the Orleans Public School System and graduated from Warren Eastern Fundamental High School.

About ten days following graduation, I enlisted and served in the United States Army. After serving my country, I returned home and served my community as a Criminal Sheriff's Deputy. On April 15, 1986, I was ordained and served the Lord as a Minister of the Gospel of Jesus Christ. However, after Hurricane Katrina, I relocated to Burleson, TX, where I founded "Making A Difference Ministries." The Ministry was about people helping people and out of that Ministry grew our live prayer line, which still takes place at 6:00 am Monday through Friday.

Fast forwarding a few years, I was honored to become a Ziglar Certified Speaker and Trainer. I believe this added depth to my ministry by giving people a plan of how to set and achieve their goals. I met Mike Rodriguez, and with the help of Tribute Publishing, I was able to become a best-selling author of my first book entitled, *Moving My Mountains - A Journey to Peace from Co-Dependency.* I was also blessed to co-author a book with a group of amazing people entitled *A Better Plan.*

My future plans include, doing everything I can, by the grace and help of God, to continue to make a difference in the lives of God's people.

Email: thegoalsman@gmail.com
Website: www.thegoalsman.com

Chapter 5 – Believe in the *You* God Created

Chapter 6

Finding Purpose
By Di-Anne Elise

Growing up in a Christian family doesn't automatically mean that you are a Christian. In my formative years I realized that God was a higher power, knowing that He is in control of everything. Knowing He is in control gives us peace only if we believe. I was 12 years old when I accepted Jesus as my Lord and Savior and even got baptized, taught Bible school to young children in my teens, and knew the Bible pretty well. As soon as my family and I moved to a different city, everything changed. We all stopped going to church and I personally strayed away from God. Thankfully, I had a praying grandmother that taught me the things to know about God.

My grandmother was a woman of God. She cared for her blind husband and her grandchildren and had a special individual relationship with all of us. After we moved to a different city, I made it a point to visit her once a week. I really admired her for her courage, perseverance, and never letting go of the things of God. I looked forward to seeing her because she was a woman of wisdom. She had lived through hard times, but she always was very optimistic and had a positive attitude. I aspired to look at life like she did, through God's lenses.

Even though I tried to look at life with God's lenses, it was not working for me at the time because I did not have a relationship with Jesus. Growing up I was a confident and intelligent girl that wanted to do the right things for herself and others. As I moved through life as a teenager and young adult, not making the best of choices but thinking that I was in control, I encountered people that I would let take a piece of my confidence a little bit at a time. When I was in my last year of high school, my mom's friend approached me and asked me what I was going to do with my life. She did not let me answer and instead proceeded to tell me that I was not college material and all I could do was get married and have babies. I was left speechless. I was shocked that she would tell me such a thing when I was always told that I could be anything that I wanted to be. I did start college, but in the back of my mind, I started thinking that maybe the lady who told me I was not college material was right. At the first good job opportunity, I dropped out of college.

I moved away from my family to pursue my new exciting job with a major airline at the age of 21 years old. I was working very hard and every chance I got. I was traveling with friends for leisure and pleasure. It was then that I met my future husband in a cosmopolitan city that had culture, wonderful food, and a lot to do for young people like me. This man was an educated man that seemed to be grounded with family, a career, and went to church every week, something that had become foreign to me. I met his family who lived in another country and before I knew it, I was married to a man eight year older than me, from another country, and a different culture, at the age of 23.

After a few years of marriage, we decided to start a family of our own and have children. As soon as I started having children, my life, marriage, and even I had changed. One may say this was expected, but my life started to change for the worse. I started to believe what that woman had told me years ago was true and I had to accept it. My self-esteem weakened, and I began to believe I had to accept everything that came my way because it was my destiny.

At that time, I had four beautiful daughters, a beautiful large house, nice cars, and lived a comfortable life. What else could I want? I remember one of my daughter's teachers would always say that it was great to be one of the girls in my family. From the outside looking in, we were the perfect family. My family members were the only ones that knew something was not right and noticed a large change in me. They saw me more uptight, wanting things to go as perfect as possible, not knowing that inside I was slowly dying. I was living life just going through the motions.

At this point I was as far away from God as possible, even though I went to church every week and was involved with the church and the girls' school activities. I kept myself busy because I did not want to think. I did not want to face what was going on, not only in my marriage, but with myself. I felt alone and had fallen into a deep depression, pretending that my life was perfect, always with a smile.

I did not realize at the time that I was in a depression because I was too busy to notice. With four girls, a demanding husband, and life, I kept myself really busy in order not to face the reality of what was going on inside of me. When the girls were school age, I would pick them up from school, go home, and take a nap. I would wake up to make dinner and take care of the girls. It felt like a vicious cycle. When my in-laws would come to visit for long periods of time because they lived in another country, the demands got greater and the air felt heavier, almost like I couldn't breathe.

If you lived in my house, you would have noticed that I was depressed. The girls were too young to notice and understand, and unfortunately in my opinion, my husband did not care. I wanted to believe there was something more to life than being a mother and a housewife. I felt like I was in jail and I didn't know what to do to get out. I felt pain, disappointment, and betrayal. I felt betrayed by myself, by my husband, and by life, but I couldn't understand why. It was almost like I was numb or if someone had placed a veil over my eyes and I couldn't see.

My family, marriage, and life were in chaos. We tried to go to counseling, but it was ineffective. It was as if my husband pretended that everything was fine and made me out to be a crazy woman. I felt dejected, disheartened, and discouraged, falling into an ever-deeper depression, all the while not knowing what was wrong with me.

One day I picked up my girls from school and was driving home when I broke down and cried so uncontrollably that I had to pull over. I panicked and couldn't believe that this was happening while all four of my daughters were in the car with me. Two were in middle school, one in elementary school, and the youngest was in pre-school. Why didn't this breakdown happen while I was alone? I couldn't stop crying. My oldest daughters kept asking me if I was ok and I couldn't even respond. When I was finally able to stop crying, I prayed and made my girls pray with me because that was the only thing I could think of that might get me out the terrible place I was in.

When I went home, I went to my room and instead of taking a nap, I simply asked God to help me. I promised that I would have a relationship with Him and I asked Him to help, lead me, and show me why I was in such a place in my life. I realized that I did not know exactly how I got to where I was. I had an idea but did not know why or how. I was always a happy, stable, and a full-of-life person before I was married and had children. What had happened to me? I was now in the quest of knowing why, and what had changed me.

I knew that arriving at an answer was going to require a lot of soul-searching and was not going to be an easy task. I decided that I was going to search for a church where I could attend by myself for a while, where I could hear the word of God without distractions or interruptions. I started visiting different weekly evening services. I found it interesting that every time I would attend a different church, I would get something different out of it. It was like God was showing and teaching me how I could listen to Him in different ways.

Several years later, we ended up in counseling again with one of my daughters. This time the counselor separated us, and it was then that I realized that something was very wrong with my marriage and everything stemmed from there. I was always taught to look at the good in people and ignore the bad, especially when it came to my husband, the head of the household. The counselor opened a part of me that had not been exposed since I was married, and I was forced to take a serious look at my life after marriage. I had changed and was not the happy-go-lucky young woman I once was. Again, I was sad, defeated, and discouraged about life. I was a woman that had lost hope in the future and was going through the motions to live life one day at a time in order not to go crazy. At the counselor's office I remember trying to soak everything in, at times in disbelief. I could not believe the extent I had ignored and neglected myself. Being totally focused on the well-being of my family, I did not pay attention to my needs in any aspect of my life (spiritually, emotionally, or psychologically). Why did I let these things happen to me? I needed to figure out why I had not realized what was going in my own life.

Like many women that marry and have children, especially if married at a young age, we tend to lose our identity. We as women get so involved in being the best wife, mother, and many things to others that we lose sight of who we are. I truly believe that we all change as we mature in life, but we have to pay attention to our well-being. It's interesting how people around you notice aspects of your life that you are not necessarily aware of as an outsider because they are looking from the outside in.

With just a few sessions, I was able to determine and make myself aware that the depression stemmed from trying to hold my family together. I was always making sure that my family was taken care of. It was determined by the counselor that I was being everything to everyone. I felt like I was the mother and the father for my children. I was always making excuses for why my husband was not present for them or why he was acting the way he was acting. I started to notice that when my husband wasn't home, the girls and I had peace, and it got to the point that I didn't want him to come home. I would try to tidy the house up and make sure the girls were ready for bed before he got home. I had become a perfectionist because I was trying my best to avoid him putting me down. I became this nervous person that drowned herself in tasks to accomplish the most perfect way possible, so we could have peace at home.

After so many years of marriage, I finally learned to calm myself down when I realized that peace came within. I found peace through Jesus who gave me comfort. And the peace of God, which surpasses all understanding will guard your hearts and your minds in Christ Jesus. (Philippians 4:7) I knew that He was guiding my steps and gave me the peace that surpassed all understanding. It was then when I was able to concentrate on myself because I knew that if I didn't, I would not be able to make sure that my daughters were going to be ok. Now it was time to follow God's plan instead of relying on my own. I came to the conclusion that my life was controlled through manipulation and mind games. It was time to work on myself and take charge of my life instead of trying to please others.

My journey started when a friend invited me to a women's Bible study. The Bible study was a wonderful start on my journey with God. I started looking for a church that we could go to as a family. When I finally found a church, my youngest girls were involved in children's ministry and my oldest were able to go to youth group. It was perfect. One

Sunday at service, I recalled sobbing tears of joy because I finally knew that my life would be on track regardless of the outcome. Whatever happened, I knew that it would be God's will "You will seek me and find me, when you seek me with all your heart" Jeremiah 29:13. I was doing my part and was confident that God would do the rest.

Now that my journey was on its way, I needed to concentrate on God's purpose in my life. I knew I had a lot to give to others but did not know how to proceed in finding my purpose. I started to search and do research on things that interested me. I had gone to college but had not finished my degree in communication, even though I had worked in the communication field. I thought to finish my degree but didn't know if I could go back to school at this point in my life. I had four children, all school age, and did not know if my demands as mother and wife would allow me to exercise this dream of mine.

As I did my research, I found out that I could complete a certification via mail as a wedding and event planner. I thought this would be right along the lines of my communication degree that I started to pursue before I got married. I was very excited. I remember discussing it with my husband and my mom. I discussed it with my mom and she was very excited and started to talk to me about putting a wedding and event business together once I got my certification. I thought it was a brilliant idea, I had someone on my side that would support me and cheer me on through the certification process.

Chapter 6 – Finding Purpose

Once I finished my certification, my mom and I started our wedding and event business. It was stressful but rewarding. Once our business started to get busier, arguments and complaints started at home. My husband discouraged me from pursuing it any further because it was taking time away from him and the girls. As a result, I agreed to give it up for the sake of my family. Having support at home was very important for me because of my daughters. I didn't want them to feel that I was not there for them, since I felt like I was the only one there for them most of the time.

When I decided to give up the business with my mom, I felt defeated, thinking that my life was useless. I had to face the fact that there was a possibility that I was not going to be able to pursue the dreams of being a productive member of society, a contributor to others that needed to experience whatever gifts and talents I had been given. I had two options: one, to give up, and the other, to keep searching and pursuing.

I was still on the hunt to exercise my gifts and talents. I distinctively remember driving my car and listening to a radio advertising about a broadcasting school that had opened a campus in my town. I thought, *maybe that is something I should pursue.* After all, I had TV experience since I had been a model, been on commercials, an extra in several movies when younger, and started a degree in the communication field when I graduated from high school. Every time I heard the commercial on the radio, I would tell myself, *maybe this is the path that I should take.* I finally got the guts to call them and through much prayer and trying to get the confidence to ask the right questions. Needless to say, they asked me to come to an audition. I was terrified; I had the fear of not performing to their standards. A few days went by and to my surprise they called me and my husband to meet the director of the broadcasting school. At this point, I did not know why they called us both, until my husband explained that he had also gone for an audition because he had always been interested in broadcasting and wanted to pursue it as a hobby. I was shocked that we both auditioned. When we met the director, I was presented with a partial scholarship to be certified in TV and radio broadcasting. I was beyond myself. But that was not all, upon completion, two of my instructors that were hosts of the morning show at a major radio station in town, offered me an internship position as an acting producer and on-air fill-in host. I couldn't believe that God was opening the door wide open for me to walk in my gift. I accepted, of course.

After five months of waking up at 3 in the morning, I had to resign my position at the radio station because I believed I did not have the proper support at home and felt my children would suffer from it. I left a position that I loved in order to keep the family together. Once again, my dreams were compromised. I knew I had to pursue what I was meant to be, but how? How could I, when I felt all alone in this journey? I remember praying to God to help me because I did not want to return to the person that I was, a person that felt hopeless and was walking around with no purpose.

As I was praying one morning, one thought came to mind, *why not go back to school and finish my bachelor's degree?* After all, I was successful at passing two certifications, and now I had more confidence in myself to pursue education after ignoring what was told about me not being cut out for college. My research began, and I stumbled upon a university that offered a bachelor's degree in communication online. I was very excited but at the same time a fear of failure came upon me. Was I capable of attending a university and successfully finishing my degree? I told myself that I would give it a try and the worst that could happen was to drop out. It was suggested that I should not attend the university because it was too late for me, I was married and had children and should not be wasting time on something that I should have done prior to getting married and having children. I was very disappointed with the feedback and with the discussions in general. I couldn't believe than once again I was not being supported and was told I was not cut out to be a college student. This shouldn't have surprised me since I've been put down because I did not have a college degree.

With a lot of prayer, I decided to go against the suggestion and pursue a bachelor's in communication. I knew that my decision was going to cause a lot of problems, but I had to stand firm because, now more than ever, I knew this was what God wanted me to do despite the obstacles I was going to be facing. I got funding on my own and started my journey as a full-time online student. There were always many disruptions the days I had papers due, tests, and a lot of schoolwork, but I knew I had to be focused and just ignore every negativity that came my way. I had a goal that I had to accomplish, and in two and a half years I finished my bachelor's degree in communications with a 3.97 average, with honors, and magna cum laude of my graduating class, which consisted of 2,000 students. I truly don't know how I reached this goal, but all I know is that without God's help I wouldn't have been able to do it. "Behold God is my helper; the Lord is the upholder of my life." (Psalm 54:4)

Chapter 6 – Finding Purpose

Now that I had a college degree, what was I going to do with it? I had always worked either in marketing or in the communication field, so I knew that I could get a job since I had experience, but now what? I had to get a job that was flexible enough, so I could take care of my family. So, I decided that I would create my own business. After all I had owned a business with my mom, and this way I could have my own hours and could dedicate as little or as much time as I wanted and build it slowly as the children grew. That is when I founded Media Resources Enterprise, a company that helped new, medium-sized businesses to create or re-create a brand and take it from developing stages to market. Despite the fact that it was not well received and accepted at home, I persevered and prevailed through every challenge I faced. I trusted that the Lord was on my side to see me through, not knowing what the turnout was going to be. "Trust in the Lord with all your heart, and do not lean on your own understanding" (Proverbs 3:5)

After three years in business and working my business very part-time because of my family demands, I was approached by a women's organization to compete in a competition for business women. The first time I was approached I was not interested and even received information via email, but I ignored it. The second time I was approached by someone recruiting for the same business women's competition, I paid some attention and became curious. At this point, I decided to approach a woman I knew that competed in pageants and asked her about this business women's competition, because if it was like a pageant, I knew it was not going to be for me, but it was worth investigating. My friend advised me that I should compete, she would sponsor me, and I would win. Apparently, it was not a pageant and there would be no bathing suit competition. I had four girls, I was a certain age, and the Lord knows that I did not want to be on a stage in a bathing suit. I decided since it was an organization that highlighted professional woman in business, something that I supported whole heartedly, I would compete, and worst-case scenario, I would meet and network with extraordinary women that would be represented nationwide.

As I prepared for the competition, the week before it began we were notified that my mother-in-law, who was battling cancer for a very long time, was in the hospital and was in her last days. She lived up north and I advised my husband to travel to see her and he did. Upon him arriving from the airport, he received a call that his mom had passed. The business woman competition was in three days. I immediately started arranging for my family, which consisted of my husband, my four girls, and myself, for our departure to where my mother-in-law lived, which meant that I would not compete. As I was trying to book flights through my husband's cousin, she could only get five tickets on Saturday and one ticket in first class on Sunday due to spring breakers trying to make their way home. The competition was on Saturday and so it seemed I was going to be in town but I had no desire to compete due to the circumstances. My husband and I discussed the possibility of me competing, and my husband insisted that I compete since I was going to be in town and I couldn't let my sponsor down. He would go ahead of me with the girls and start arrangements. He assured me that nothing would be happening until Monday anyways. I agreed to compete in the business women's competition despite my hesitation.

Needless to say, that while in the competition I was going through the motions. I felt like I was floating on air. The competition consisted of a panel interview that was worth 40% and thank God I was used to public speaking so I didn't have to think; it came natural to me. At the end of the competition there was an onstage question. Apparently, Mrs. California and I were neck and neck and I did not know this could have been a tie breaker. I had never competed in any type of competition, so at this time I was clueless of what was going on. All I can remember was the onstage question they asked me, "Who is your role model and why?" I responded that here on earth was my grandmother that showed me the things of God, but ultimately my role model was my higher power, my God that strengthens me. I walked back to my post next to Mrs. California, this apparently was not her first rodeo, because she grabbed my hand and whispered in my ear, "You won." I looked at her in confusion, thinking, *how does she know?* Shortly after the judges where breaking the tie, they announced me as the new Mrs. Corporate America. I was in shock! I felt someone push me to walk so I could be crowned and announced as the winner. I did not go to sleep that night. I packed and went straight to the airport to catch up with my family. God was in control. I was even flying first class to catch up with my family.

Acquiring the title of Mrs. Corporate America allowed me to reach so many women in order to tell my story from depression to triumph through Jesus Christ. I have been in many interviews with the media and it even landed me a spot on the five o'clock news as the expert in marketing and advertising and many other wonderful opportunities. My business exploded at that time and I was able to help many business owners and mid-size businesses. But with that said, my home life was getting worse. At this point I buried myself in work and made sure my girls were taken care of. I decided that I would write a book since my life was not busy enough.

My book writing required time, but I was determined to be obedient to what God was assigning me to do. My professional heart has always been for entrepreneurs. I knew in my heart that God had called me to help them develop their professional purpose (Jeremiah 29:11). I found a publishing company that would allow me to retain the rights of the book and off I went with publishing my first book. The Lord was guiding my every step for His will. The book was published a year later. That year was one of the best years in my professional career. I found so much joy in helping get small businesses ready for market and now they had a resource that will help them in that process other than me.

Even though my marriage did not work out and I became a single mother of 2 college students and 2 daughters at home, God has blessed me beyond measure. Finding my purpose has allowed me to be fulfilled in my professional and personal life. Living God's purpose in your life is the most rewarding blessing that anyone could have. Follow your gifts, that will allow you to manifest your talents that will lead you to your purpose. Peace and may God bless you through my story. If you like my chapter, make sure to visit my website at www.dianneelise.com for upcoming books.

About the Author – Di-Anne Elise

Di-Anne Elise, founder of Media Resources Enterprise, is a business communication author, speaker, coach and trainer in the areas of branding, public relations, marketing and social media strategy. She is also the founder of Global Partners Resources Foundation, the former National Association of Professional Women (NAPW) Public Relations woman of the year, the recipient of the WOAMTEC Community Leadership Award, Mrs. Corporate America and the reigning Ms. Corporate America Lifetime Queen. Di-Anne has the expertise professionalism, and people skills to help businesses communicate to the public. She obtained a bachelor's degree in Communication with concentration in Public Relations, and Marketing, graduating Magna Cum Laude from Ashford University. She has a professional broadcasting certification for Radio/TV from the Connecticut School of Broadcasting, and a news contributor for WOFL Fox 35 TV Orlando, FL. She assists communication campaigns to promote her client's interests in the areas of branding, public relations, and marketing.

Di-Anne's passion is to empower businesses and individuals to achieve best results through public communication.

Chapter 6 – Finding Purpose

To arrange speaking engagements, book signings, tour events, interviews, online chats, telephone chats, webinars, or telecasts contact Di-Anne Elise at:

Dianne@mediaresourcesenterprise.com

or visit online at

www.mediaresourcesenterprise.com

for more information.

Chapter 6 – Finding Purpose

Chapter 7

Rock Bottom and out Again
By Jeremy A. Almond

Like most police officers can attest to, the journey on becoming an officer and staying true to your values can be a bumpy road. They tell you in the academy the first few days to watch out for the three "B's." They are booze, broads, and bills. These are the top three things which get so many cops in trouble during their career. When you first go through initial training, you tell yourself you are never going to be one of "those cops." You know who I'm talking about. The cop who comes to work still smelling like last weekend. The cop who is going on his fourth marriage. The cop who is always at the payday loan store down the road from your squad's favorite coffee shop.

I was just like any other recruit, I suppose. Although unlike other recruits, five months prior, I had just graduated from infantry training at Fort Benning, Georgia. I had joined the Army National Guard with the hope it would help me get hired faster into law enforcement. I had signed the papers in 2004, and I didn't go to Army Basic Training until winter 2005. During this time, it was well known that if you were signing up, you were going to Iraq or Afghanistan. But I told myself *to hell with it*. If it would help me get a leg up during the police testing, then it was a risk worth taking. Little did I know I was laying all the groundwork for the next 14 years of the best, worst, horrific, and greatest time of my life. One that had me lose my faith, but finally begin to walk with God again.

Let us start at the beginning. Before I had enlisted with the military, I was working as a security guard in a large mall. I have to admit I was having fun. Probably the best fun I had working at a job. During that time, I was near the end of my involvement as a police cadet. I had been a cadet for around five years at that point. As a cadet, I learned everything I ever wanted about my dream career. I also knew that without college or military experience, it would be difficult to maneuver into a position where I could be competitive.

Since I was not quite 21 yet, I could not apply for the patrol position I wanted. I was told I could attempt to get an age waiver from the civil service commission and apply for a corrections position. I was told this could help get my foot in the door. I knew quite a few deputies as a cadet who had previously been corrections officers. So I said to myself, why not? I applied for and was granted the age waiver. I had the support of quite a few supervisors. So I have a waiver to apply for, now what? Next, I took the written test and the physical test. The physical test wasn't too bad, even for a husky guy like me. By husky, I mean slightly overweight. I barely made it past the written. But, I still scored an interview. The time came for the interview. I was very nervous. I was sweating even before I got into my car. I made my way over to the office and was brought into the conference room. I had been there many times as a cadet. Still, even being familiar with the room and knowing the people in front of me, I was frightened. I could feel my face filling with blood. I imagined if the power were to have gone out, we could still do the interview with the glow off of my head.

After the interview was done and I walked out, I actually felt really good about it. I found out later I did not get the position because I didn't have any credit history. I was very upset about something so minuscule compared to what I had done to prepare. Did they expect me to have an 800 credit score at my age? Maybe some people at my age had this going for them. I definitely never focused on it. I never had a credit card. I simply worked to pay the small amount of bills I did have.

I went back and continued to work the night shift at the mall. I tried to figure out what to do with my life as I walked up and down the empty storefronts. The only exciting thing during this time was that I could change the mall speakers to play my favorite music. Ah, the perks to being the only one in a giant mall! I don't think the mall manager would have approved of my type of music blasted throughout his entire facility.

It was around this time a friend of mine began walking along the corridors with me to pass the time at night. I had told him everything that happened in the interview. He told me he was joining the United States Army National Guard. And it just so happened there was a recruiting station in the mall. With him talking it up and my series of recent events, I felt joining the military must have to happen. Besides, what else was I going to do with my life? I had still not finished college, I was not 21 yet, and not in the best shape. I felt I was meant to accomplish something more. Something bigger than writing tickets to shop owners who didn't open up on time.

My family is full of prior military and law enforcement. I wanted to avoid having to join the military. To be frank, I was scared. The concept of going through the rigorous training and the very real possibility of going to war shook me to my core. I did not have confidence in myself at all. This was also in 2004, just three years after September 11th, 2001 and our entry into Afghanistan and Iraq thereafter. I knew once I signed on the dotted line, I would be headed over in some capacity. As I thought about it, I was convinced it would help me get hired on back at the Sheriff's Office where I was a cadet. At least, that is what I told myself.

September 13th, 2004, I officially signed into the United States Army. I took my oath at the Seattle MEPS (Military Entrance Processing Station) with several others. The MOS (Military Occupation Specialty) I picked was infantry. You must be thinking to yourself, "This guy has been talking about how scared he was about making it in the military, and he chose infantry!?" I will admit, my parents were not thrilled about me joining the military, let alone that particular job. In fact, I believed my grandmother cried, my father yelled at me, and my mother about fainted. I am pretty confident if my sister were present during all three reactions, she would have had a bowl of popcorn.

Chapter 7 – Rock Bottom and out Again

So, it was done. I ended up reporting to Fort Benning, Georgia, right before winter came through in 2005. I graduated in February 2006 and headed back home. It was during my time at Basic Training, where I began to attend church regularly. Every Sunday I would go to the service. I began reading the Bible at night, knowing God was there to guide me through every step of the way. I truly believed Jesus was the son of the living God. I got baptized there at Fort Benning.

When I got back to Washington State, I walked into the Sheriff's Office and spoke with a member of the administration. I was fresh out of Basic Training and in my army uniform. I told him I wanted a job, a Patrol Deputy position. He looked around his desk, paperwork all over. He then looked back up and said, "You got it. You just gotta take the test." I left ecstatic. I took the tests and came out 2nd, just a few points behind number one. Luckily, by the time I was done with the testing, there were now two slots open. I was hired in May 2006. I then went to law enforcement basic training in July 2006.

I struggled for the first year and a half to two years. I was 22 when I started in law enforcement. I was very young and did not have much in the way of life experience. In 2007 I left for what was called "Operation Cobra Gold." It was a short deployment to Thailand for training one on one with my infantry counterparts. The last two days we got to spend in Bangkok. I will save those stories for another book.

After we got back and some time had passed, my National Guard unit was alerted about a deployment to Iraq. I knew this time would come; I expected it. It was still a kick to the gut. I knew my parents and grandparents were going to lose their ever-loving minds. But they knew what I signed up for and why. They knew it was a sacrifice I wanted to make if it meant I got into law enforcement.

Before I left for pre-mobilization in August 2008, I had been seeing a woman who I fell in love with. I knew there was a possibility I would not be coming back. I wrote and sealed several letters and left them in the hands of a trusted friend. I proposed to the woman. I told her I would be coming back. What I didn't know was the condition in which I would be coming back in. I remember the embrace we had, the tears while sitting in the parking lot as she dropped me off. From there, I spent three months at two different bases before hitching a plane ride to Kuwait.

We stayed in Kuwait for several weeks to get acclimated to the climate. This meant sweating every second of the day and night while drinking the most amount of water I have had in my life. From there, we flew north. I got off the plane in Iraq late at night. As soon as the ramp dropped, the smell of burning garbage filled my nostrils. I looked out at the flat scenery and thought, "What the hell did I get myself into?" The next nine months changed me forever. I quickly found out the base I was now stationed at was nicknamed "Mortaritaville." It definitely lived up to its name. Just about every morning from 1am-4am we would have mortars fired by insurgents from outside the base into different areas of the base.

The first few weeks were terrifying. Not only did we begin running convoy operations every few days, but the sounds of mortars coming in every night kept me up. I would stay up wondering if one of them was going to ever land in my room. The days turned into weeks, the weeks into months. I was beginning to sleep through the night, ignoring the distant explosions. I noticed things were starting to change with how I acted, but I never thought twice about it until later. I disregarded the danger of where I was at. Those pesky insurgents were never able to reach me. I was invincible! That is, until one night.

Fortunately, I had another Deputy I worked with deploy with my unit. I was able to convince him to come out of the army reserves and into my National Guard unit. He wanted to go overseas anyway so I didn't feel too bad about it. He was living nearby my small room I shared with another guy. I then heard and felt a loud explosion. This one was different. Could it have been an insurgent who actually got closer to the fence this time? Unlikely. It was closer but still did not feel as if it was really close. As I sat there, I heard another one. This time a little bit louder. A little bit more shaking.

This one was definitely close. I got under my bed and grabbed my body armor. Silence. Then another explosion, louder than the last two. This felt closer. Really close. I was frantically trying to cover myself with the body armor and anything else I could find. BOOM. Another one. The fourth one felt like it was right outside my door. It was at this point I knew the next one would be coming through my ceiling. I waited for my demise. Life flashed before my eyes; all the mistakes I ever made, all of the people I ever loved, all the things I wanted to tell my parents but never did.

Chapter 7 – Rock Bottom and out Again

I waited for what felt like an eternity. It was completely quiet. Then I began hearing yelling. Four, small rockets had landed all within 300 meters of my living space. Two hit my unit's motorpool (the area where we park our armored vehicles). One hit the dirt road outside my living area, and the fourth hit the inside of a concrete wall which shot debris into a living unit several doors down from me. Luckily, the guy who lived in there was on leave at the time of the explosion.

Here are two other defining moments during my time in Iraq.

During a convoy mission, I was hit by what is referred to as an IED or improvised explosive device. I was driving our vehicle over a bridge in north Baghdad. I don't remember what we were talking about before the detonation, but I do remember the bright flash and the feeling of air pressure hitting my body. Once I realized what happened, I sped up, not knowing if I had any wheels or the status of my gunner behind me. Luckily for us, it was what they called a shape charge IED. This meant there was a copper plate in the tube which turns into a large bullet. They had mounted it wrong, and it fired straight up instead of into our vehicle.

While on another mission, we were convoying from one base to another. Our convoys were always at night. Sometimes we drove with our headlights blacked out and navigated by other means. As I was driving, I saw a bright flash of light against the palm trees out in the distance. As this happened, I heard a loud explosion. Just then, a burst of radio traffic sounded over my headset. An IED had just hit one of the trucks behind me. We blacked out our lights and turned around. I drove towards the area of the blast. I then saw a figure diving down on the other side of a pole on the ground.

This moment would play through my mind over and over as the years went on. At the time, it felt like a videogame. The screen I was looking at was directly in front of my face. As I called out the position of the suspected insurgent to my gunner, I saw rounds from the machine gun hitting the downed pole. The bullets were bouncing off of it. It was then I began registering what was on my screen as hot chunks began flying up from where the insurgent had jumped to. I continued to tell my gunner to keep on target. It wasn't until hot brass began going down my neck that I realized this was not a videogame; it was actually happening.

The rest of my deployment would see similar scenes of war. Almost daily were incoming mortars into our base, there was anxiety every other day of going out on mission, not knowing if you are going to come back in one piece or many. As the months went on, we got closer and closer to the day where we finally got to go home. For two of the guys in my platoon, they would be coming back severely injured. Several weeks before we got to go home, there was one mission where I did not have to go out with my platoon. I remember running around the track late at night as this was usually our time to be up. I saw a helicopter come in flying to the hospital on our base. That was never a good sign.

I soon found out as word spread that my platoon's convoy had been hit again. This time, the driver's middle fingers were taken out. The sergeant in the passenger seat received severe injuries from the shape charge IED skimming the front dashboard and exploding on the inside of the passenger door from shrapnel against everyone inside the front cab. Visiting the two of them in the hospital was heart-wrenching. They would soon be flown out and headed back home.

We then flew back home in August 2009. I remember meeting the governor again on the plane when we landed. In all honesty, I didn't want to go through any ceremony or other spectacular event to mark the occasion. I wanted to go directly home and lay in my own bed. Home, where I didn't have to worry about explosions and gunfire. A lot of things changed in law enforcement during the time my partner and I were gone. They had planned on giving us new patrol cars, which were waiting for us when we would eventually come back to work. We were reconnecting with friends and family, both close personal friends and other coworkers.

I did not plan on going back to work for some time. I needed to have a long transition before I ventured back into the dangerous job I had before I left for overseas. I then got a phone call that no police officer ever wants to get. Around 8:30 PM on August 17, 2009, Deputy Stephen Michael Gallagher was on his way to back-up one of our other deputies near a small town in the south foothills of Mount Rainier. Deputy Gallagher collided with an elk which was on the highway. After hearing the information, I gathered up some things and traveled up north to Seattle to Harborview Medical Center, where I was told he was going to be flown to.

When I showed up to the hospital, I saw some of the deputies I had not seen since I worked with them in 2008. I remember walking into the hallway outside of the emergency room where Mike was. The sheriff was holding a binder. He looked so heartbroken, exhausted, and many other emotions all at once. Mike and I had worked together before I left. I always remember his smile and his upbeat and positive attitude towards life. I prepared myself as I walked into the emergency room where he was being worked on. While I will not share what was said or seen in that emergency room, I will tell you that was one of the most difficult things I've ever had to go through my entire life. He succumbed to his injuries the following day.

After talking with administration officials, I picked up my new patrol car, gathered all my uniforms and equipment, and went back up to Harborview. I stood watch with his casket as we prepared to escort him back home from Seattle. The procession from Seattle South along Interstate 5 was quiet. As we were leaving Seattle, the entire roadway was lined with Seattle police officers, firefighters, and paramedics along with civilians saluting. As we traveled through Seattle and back onto the freeway to head south, the scene was the same at just about every overpass on the way home. I could not stop crying. I was overwhelmed with emotions.

After the funeral service, I went back to work. This set into motion things I've been working on ever since. There were times where I would find myself driving my patrol car down the middle of the highway to avoid IEDs. I was skittish around gunfire in the distance. My irritability and patience with people became horrible. In the few months that I was back home and back to work, I got married to the woman I was engaged to before I left for Iraq. We bought a new house and a truck. Eventually, my wife became pregnant with my first child.

I thought that I could handle all of the stress and anger that had been accumulating by myself. This eventually led to my wife moving out with our son and getting a divorce. I had to get rid of my truck and sell the house because I couldn't afford these things any more by myself. I was also now getting in trouble at work because of my irritability. I found myself having a hard time trying to stop drinking. I was using drinking to cope with everything that had been going on. I was becoming another statistic. They tell you about all this in the Academy. But I was young and naïve. I knew at the time, with all my training and experience, along with watching other people go through it, that I would not end up being that statistic. I was brutally wrong.

I eventually met another woman who I married. But as time went on with this new change in my life, I was still not able to shake everything that I'd been doing to myself and others. I had seen counselors on and off but never really stuck to any schedule. More importantly, I was not turning to God. I had not really been to church or had a conversation Him since I was baptized back in 2006. My wife would try and get me to go to church, but I would politely decline or make myself busy with other things. Was it because I was ashamed to go to church and be judged? Was it because I felt I wasn't deserving of His love? There were many reasons I kept finding not to go.

Chapter 7 – Rock Bottom and out Again

Everything culminated into a policy violation at work in mid-2017. This policy violation saw me get stripped of all of my specialty positions that I worked so hard to get. While I still have some disagreement about how it was handled, the damage was already done. A few months later, I was hit with another minor policy violation. I was getting angry with everyone and felt as though people were out to get me. I began stepping out on my marriage, which ultimately led me to decide to keep fighting or leaving the job entirely. I left the job that I loved so dearly, but I knew it was really no one else's fault but mine. I also had to grapple with my wife moving out and how I was going to try and repair my marriage.

I was at rock bottom. Even though I was at rock bottom, I felt like I kept trying to shovel my way further down. It wasn't until I started going back to counseling and eventually began walking back into my church that things began turning around. I ended up being diagnosed with PTSD (Post Traumatic Stress Disorder). At that point, I put all my trust in God to help me realize what was going on. After leaving my job, I took a leap of faith and started my own business, which I still run today.

All of the positive things that have happened to me post law-enforcement life are because of my faith in God. Things began happening quickly. They only started to come together so quickly because I had been getting more involved with my church. Around this same time came an even bigger bombshell. My wife was now pregnant. We had been trying for many years to conceive. How could it be, at this moment in our lives, that God decided this was for the better?

Chapter 7 – Rock Bottom and out Again

Bringing a child into the environment I had created for my family was not something I thought I would be able to get through. I was extremely excited about having another child. I was also as equally scared of how I would explain this part of our life story down the road to my child. I did not want to make the wrong choice in anything else I did from this point out.

I had many discussions with our Pastor and how God was testing me. What I came to realize in talking with him was God needed me to go through those trials so I would come out of it as the person my family needed me to be. Who God wanted me to be. My business was, in the bigger picture, the smallest thing to happen. The biggest positive change was who I was evolving into. I was evolving into a man. No longer a young, foolish boy with no self-control, I was a man who became the loving husband to his wife. A man who became the father his children needed. A man who would show his own parents he was able to go through all of that and come out a son they were even more proud of. A man who God would still love no matter what, but maybe, just maybe, give me that "wink," the acknowledgment I want to believe I received for following His will. No matter what was happening this past year, I would listen to Him. I would pray about the decisions I had to make. I prayed to Him to give me guidance on what He wanted me to do, and the strength in which to carry it out.

I knew turning to Him and trusting in His infinite wisdom was much better than trying to do things on my own. He has a plan for all of us. If you sit down and have a conversation with Him, he will guide you on the right path.

Do I still deal with PTSD? Yes. But I thank Him and my beautiful wife for sticking by my side through my dark journey back into the light. Without her love and God's love for me, I would not be blessed with my now three beautiful children.

I know in my heart what happened with my previous life was His wake-up call for me to change course. No matter what you have done in your life, no matter how many hearts you have broken or how much damage you have done, He will always be right there next to you ready to forgive. I wish I could take everything back, I really do, but I can't. None of us can. Only Jesus can wipe away your past to make you right again. It is what we learn from it that makes us better human beings. It is the blind faith in God you must have to help steer your life, your journey. After all, you never know when God may come calling to bring you home.

About the Author – Jeremy Almond

Mr. Jeremy Almond is a decorated 12-year law enforcement veteran. He was a Deputy before getting promoted to Detectives. While in Detectives, he worked major investigations, but his primary focus was child crimes. During this time, he was also assigned to the regional critical incident investigation team (CIIT) which incorporated five counties. Its focus was primarily officer involved shootings. He was also the county's Gang Task Force Coordinator. He also had assignments with Honor Guard, Field Training Officer, Cadet Coordinator, Assistant Reserve Deputy Coordinator and at the time SERT (Sheriff's Emergency Response Team) heavy vehicle operator. He is the recipient of over 20 awards and letters of appreciation.

During this time in law enforcement, he was also in the United States Army National Guard. His job was as an Infantryman. He was deployed for Operation Iraqi Freedom in 2008-2009 and Operation Cobra Gold 2007. He has received numerous medals and accommodations during his military career including the combat infantry badge for his actions in Iraq. His vehicle was struck by an IED (Improvised Explosive Device) in Iraq which has caused him to have tinnitus to this day. While serving in the military and law enforcement he also volunteered on his days off as a firefighter for the fire district he lived in.

Since May 2018, Mr. Almond opened and runs his own licensed private investigative agency in Washington State. He assists citizens with their cases while also auditing police reports they provide and conducting surveillance. His business is also a licensed training provider for the American Red Cross. As an instructor he teaches several first aid classes a month.

Mr. Almond can be contacted through his website at:

www.gadsdenrisk.com
or
www.facebook.com/gadsdenrisk.

Final Thoughts by Mike Rodriguez

Throughout my life, I have always felt a bigger and better plan for my life, but I have not always been in pursuit of it, mostly because I have been my biggest obstacle. I was often distracted by my current comfort zones through my current routines. They kept me from stepping into my full potential and kept me bound, as a prisoner of mediocrity. I knew that I wanted to pursue my "purpose," I just wasn't focused enough to see it or empowered enough to take action.

After years of very strong feelings that God had something more for me, I only took action to start changing my life, when I chose to have faith and act on God's plan for me. I knew this was the only way to make big changes in my life. Through His grace, I am a new man. I understand my purpose and I am full of life. I can see Him clearly, and I am stronger than ever.

With regard to purpose, I have always felt that mine was to help others through the gift of speaking. I have always dreamed of becoming a motivational/inspirational speaker, or maybe even a preacher, but for the largest part of my life, I only considered this a dream.

Who was I to do these things?

What credentials or gifts did I have?

These were negative thoughts that I burdened myself with.

So, who am I?

I am a son of our King.

I know Him and He knows me.

Today, all because of Him, and through my obedience to decide, take action and have faith, I am continuing to live my life's dream. I am pursuing my life's goal, and most importantly, my life's purpose to help others build their lives all for the glory of God. Not only do I travel and speak full-time, but I am also pursuing my MDiv at SWBTS to preach around the world.

Believe in God and accept Him and His calling for your life. Have faith and act. You too can realize how to live beyond purpose as the son or daughter of the same King!

Now Go Forth and Make YOUR Life Exceptional!

-   **Mike Rodriguez**

About Mike Rodriguez

Mike Rodriguez is a professional speaker, a master trainer and a global evangelist. He is CEO of Mike Rodriguez International, LLC, a professional speaking, training and global ministry organization. Besides being a Best-Selling author, he is a highly sought-after motivator and a leadership, change, and sales expert. Mike and his wife Bonnie also own a publishing company and they still manage to spend quality time with their five daughters, all while Mike is studying for his Master's Degree (MDiv) and for an Advanced Certificate of Ministry from Truett Seminary at Baylor University. Mike previously studied at DTS (in 2017), and at SWBTS (2018) and an Oxford Study abroad program in 2019.

Mike is a former showcase speaker with the original Zig Ziglar Corporation and was selected as their key speaker for the 2015 Ziglar U.S. Tour.

Mike delivers performance-based seminars and trainings and has authored several books which have been promoted by Barnes & Noble. He has been featured on CBS, U.S. News & World Report, Success Magazine, Fast Company and Business Insider. He has lectured at Baylor University, UNT, K-State Research, Louisiana tech, and UGA. His clients include names like Hilton, Bank of America, McDonald's Corporation, the U.S. Army, and the Federal Government. As a people expert, Mike has trained thousands around the world.

Everyone faces challenges; Mike believes that through faith and action, you can overcome the challenges in your life to attain your goals and become who God has called you to be.

Mike has been happily married since 1991 to Bonnie, the love of his life and together they have five beautiful daughters.

As a highly sought-after speaker, trainer, and advisor,
Mike has experience working with people
from all walks of life.

You can schedule Mike Rodriguez
to speak, inspire or train at your next event.
Go to:
www.MikeRodriguezInternational.com

Other products available by Mike Rodriguez:

Finding Your WHY
8 Keys to Exceptional Selling
Break Your Routines to Fix Your Life
NOW Is the Best Time
Lion Leadership
Think BIG Motivational Quotes

Walking with Faith
A Bigger Purpose
A Journey to Hope
Trusting in Him
A Better Plan

What's Holding me Back?
(Audio Course from Nightingale Conant)

Disclaimer & Copyright Information

*"I can do ALL THINGS through Christ
who strengthens me."
Philippians 4:13*

NOTES

NOTES

CPSIA information can be obtained
at www.ICGtesting.com
Printed in the USA
BVHW072351120819
555662BV00007B/939/P